MARITIME
SCOTLAND

Printed and bound in Spain by
Bookprint, S. L., Barcelona

Published by
B.T. Batsford Ltd
9 Blenheim Court
Brewery Road
A member of the Chrysalis Group plc

A catalogue record for this book is available from the British library

ISBN 0 7134 8520 5

HISTORIC ✠ SCOTLAND

MARITIME SCOTLAND

BRIAN LAVERY

B. T. Batsford Ltd • Historic Scotland

Contents

Illustrations

Colour Plates

Acknowledgements

Thanks are due to: Don Hind and the crew of *Lorne Leader* for first inspiring me to study the subject; David Breeze of Historic Scotland; Jim Tildesley and Ian Wyper of the Scottish Maritime Museum; Iain Mackenzie, Alisdair Macleod, Bob Todd, Hugh Murphy (former Caird Fellow) formerly of the National Maritime Museum; Robert Prescott of the Scottish Institute of Maritime Studies and the Scottish Fisheries Museum; John Edwards of Aberdeen Maritime Museum; Jock Gardiner of the Naval Historical Branch, Whitehall; Chris Howard Bailey of the Royal Naval Museum, Portsmouth; Lewis Johnman of the University of Westminster; Roderick Stewart of HMS *Unicorn*; Vice-Admiral Sir Roderick MacDonald RN; Commodore Duncan Ellin RN; Len Paterson of Glenlight Shipping; the staffs of the London Library, Public Record Office, Scottish Record Office, and Strathclyde Regional Archives.

The following individuals and institutions provided, and in most cases hold the copyright for, the illustrations: Crown Copyright: HM Naval Base Clyde, Faslane (117); Forth Ports plc (2); Glasgow Museums: Art Gallery and Museum (1); Fife Council Museums: Methil Heritage Centre (58); Historic Scotland (1, 4B, 5B, 7, 8, 13, 15L, 19, 21, 22T, 22B, 27, 35, 41, 42, 51, 53, 54, 57L, 57R, 60, 62, 64, 67, 68, 69, 74, 78, 80, 82, 83, 86, 88, 94, 99, 102, 104, 108, 112, 115T, 115B); Hunterian Museum & Art Gallery (14); Imperial War Museum (4T); Brian Lavery (3, 36, 40, 70); MacLean Museum, Inverclyde Council (2, 38, 39, 55); National Archives of Scotland (71B); National Maritime Museum (3, 19T, 31, 33, 34, 37, 43, 44, 48, 66, 71T, 72, 76, 77, 84, 87, 89, 90, 92, 96, 100, 103, 109, 116); Public Record Office (106B, 107); Royal Commission on the Ancient & Historical Monuments of Scotland (RCAHMS) (6, 25, 29, 50); Science & Society (52); Scottish Highland Photo Library (89B); Scottish National Portrait Gallery (28).

Author's Note

Miles and the original tonnage of ships are kept in the original measures, as these remain standard. Knots are still in common use; 1 knot equals 1.15 miles per hour. Where sizes are mainly used for comparison, for example 15 inch guns in Chapter 5, the imperial measures are also retained. In other cases, the metric equivalent is given when appropriate.

Introduction

The people of Scotland have always been close to the sea. It is impossible to live more than 40 miles from salt water except on the heights of the Cairngorms. The sea forms most of the boundaries of Scotland, though these have not always been fixed – in the past the Western Isles have been ruled from Ireland and Norway, Orkney and Shetland by Norway. Sea transport has always had a vital role in holding the country together, across its innumerable lochs, rivers, channels and sounds. It has also opened up the possibilities of international trade, allowing Scotland to develop relations with many places without going through its old rival, England.

Nearly a third of Scotland's population lives in the four great cities, Glasgow, Edinburgh, Dundee and Aberdeen, all of which are seaports; though this was not achieved without some effort, for Edinburgh had to create a satellite port at Leith, while Glasgow used enormous resources in deepening the Clyde. The cultural difference between Edinburgh and Glasgow is great for two cities so close together. This is partly explained by the fact that they face in different directions – Edinburgh towards England and the Continent, Glasgow towards Ireland,

the Western Isles and America.

Throughout the centuries Scotland has maintained independent relations with Scandinavia, the Netherlands, Ireland, France and North America. According to Professor Donaldson:

'From the Firth of Forth, Bremen and Bergen are no further away than Antwerp and Dieppe; from Aberdeen, the Kattegat is as near as the English Channel and the nearest continental country is Norway.'

Without the maritime dimension, England is seen as Scotland's only neighbour and that country seems to dominate Scotland's history.

This book attempts to take an overall view of Scottish maritime history, archaeology and building and monuments, uniting the different themes of passenger and cargo shipping, fishing, shipbuilding and naval history, each of which is well covered by its own specialists, with little reference to how it relates to the others. Because of pressures of space, it is regrettably not possible to do full justice to all aspects of the subject – yachting, the seaside, lifeboats and shipwrecks, for example, are barely mentioned (but see Colin Martin's *Scotland's Historic Shipwreck*s in this series).

1
Early History

Prehistoric peoples

The earliest people in Scotland were even closer to the sea than their descendants. The area was virtually uninhabited, except perhaps for isolated groups of hunters, until the end of the last Ice Age about 10,000 BC. After that, people may have arrived simply by trekking north from what later became England. Others could have come from the east without crossing water, for they may have lived in a plain which occupied the area now covered by the North Sea, and simply moved on as the ice melted and water covered their lands. They brought a version of Scandinavian culture and techniques into Scotland. There is also evidence that the earliest settlers came from Ireland, and they certainly must have used boats. Of 11 settlements known to be more than 7800 years old, seven are on Hebridean islands, two are on the west coast of the mainland and one is on an inland loch (1).

Prehistoric Scotland was a land of forests, mountains, marshes, lochs and unbridged rivers, with no roads or wheeled transport. Boats provided the means of getting about by sea and river, either for families and clans in permanent or seasonal migrations, for hunters in search of new areas, or for getting raw materials, such as the stone of Arran for making tools. Boats were also essential for certain types of fishing, which was certainly one of the main activities of early people in Scotland. The shell mounds of Oronsay, used approximately 5500 years ago, contain the refuse of a society which was heavily

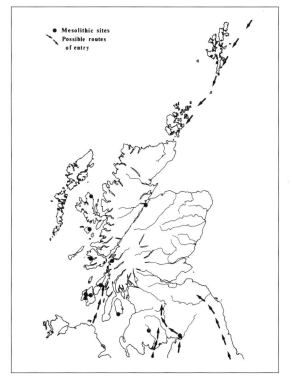

1 The routes that the first settlers may have taken to Scotland, and the mesolithic sites more than 7800 years old, all close to the sea or lochs.

dependent on the sea for its food.

We know very little about the boats used by the earliest settlers. Developments elsewhere in Europe suggest that the dug-out canoe was possible and remains of several have been found in Scotland, though none can definitely be dated from this period. The skin boat, with a wooden frame, is another possibility, as paintings and carvings of such craft have been found in Scandinavia.

The most striking buildings of the period between 100 BC and 100 AD, the brochs, are invariably situated close to the sea. About 500 have been identified and they are common in the treeless environments of the western Highlands, Caithness and the Northern and Western Isles. The people who built them must have used the sea themselves, and may have feared attack from it.

Crannogs also belong to this period and are even more closely connected with the water, if not the sea. Most are artificial lake dwellings, which offered some protection against wild animals and bands of robbers. A few, for example at Dumbuck in the Clyde and Loch Spelve in Mull, were built in estuaries or sea-lochs where the rise of the tide was not too great. Crannogs were also built throughout the Middle Ages.

The Romans

For a long time, Scotland was beyond the range of the civilisations of the Middle East and Mediterranean, which spread westward by Phoenician trade and Roman conquest. However Pytheas of Marseilles led an expedition to the area around 325 BC, where he was informed of Thule 'six days north of Britain ... near the Frozen Cronian sea.' Others followed and the information was eventually incorporated in Ptolemy's map of around 140 AD, which showed Scotland running from west to east but which includes many identifiable place-names.

The Romans, who began their conquest of southern Britain in 43 AD, have a reputation as landlubbers, but they employed galleys with some success in co-operation with land forces (2). Thus, in AD 82 or 83 the Governor of Britain, Julius Agricola, sent an expedition up the north-east coast of Scotland, beyond the Forth. According to Tacitus:

'The war was pushed forward simultaneously by land and sea; and infantry, cavalry and marines, often meeting in the same camp, would mess and make merry together. They would boast, as soldiers will, of their several exploits and adventures, and match the perilous depths of woods and mountains against the hazards of storms and tides, the victory on land against the conquest of the ocean. The Britons, for their part, were stupefied by the appearance of the fleet.'

The Roman fleet, the *Classis Britannicus*, was based in Kent and consisted of galleys of far greater military power than anything the Caledonians and their successors the Picts could produce.

The Scots and the coracle

By the fourth century AD, the Roman frontier was crumbling and Irish raiders were attacking the west of Scotland. One of their victims was St Patrick, who was captured and taken to Ireland where, as we know, he helped the spread of Christianity. By 500 AD the original Scots, natives of the north of Ireland, had set up the kingdom of Dal Rìata in what is now Argyll.

In 563 Columba, an Irish monk of princely descent, arrived in the Western Isles with a mission to spread Christianity among the Picts to the east and north of Dal Rìata. He chose the island of Iona as his headquarters, not because he wanted isolation like his medieval succes-

2 A Roman coin of 205 AD, found in Scotland, showing a galley.

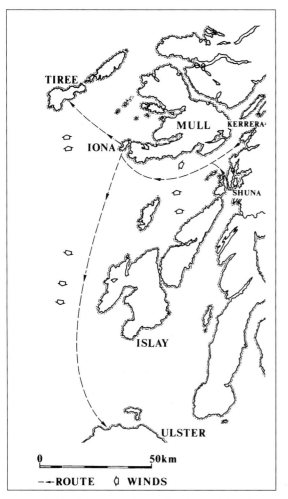

3 Some of Columba's voyages showing the winds used, based on Adamnan.

4 The prow of the Oseberg ship, a Viking ship excavated in Norway in 1904 and now on display in Oslo.

sors, but because it was the centre of an area of sea from which he could communicate with his home in Donegal, the Hebrides, and mainland Scotland. Like his kinsmen who had founded Dal Rìata, he used the curragh, a boat of perhaps 15 to 25 ft (4.6 to 7.6 m) long, constructed from leather stretched on a wooden frame.

Columba's biographer, Adamnan, gives some clues to the sailing qualities of such vessels, usually in the context of miracles attributed to the Saint. They could be rowed in calm weather, but in a tempest they might be 'violently tossed and shaken with the huge dashing waves'. They could not sail much, if at all, into the wind, because they had very little under the water to stop them being blown sideways (3). A south-easterly was 'most favourable' to carry them from Kerrera to Iona, basically a westerly voyage, in which the sailors 'were directed to raise the sail yards in the form of a cross, and spread the sails upon them' – implying that some other arrangement, perhaps similar to lug sails, was more common. Also with a favourable wind, it was possible to sail from Shuna to Iona (about 17 miles) in less than three hours – a speed which would be quite acceptable to modern yachtsmen. The monks also used 'long boats of hewn pine and oak' which could be drawn over land.

The Viking age

In 795 Iona was looted and the people of the Western Isles began to feel the effects of a race who moved across the seas with even greater skill than the Irish and Scots. The classic Viking ship had already evolved among the fjords and rivers of northern Europe, where sea transport was even more vital than in western Scotland. The Norsemen too had begun with skin boats, but by 600 AD they had evolved a wooden boat, made from overlapping planks in a system which is known as clinker-build. We know a great deal about them because of three major ship burials in Norway and five ships from around 1000 AD which were sunk at Roskilde in Denmark (4).

Unlike earlier craft they had a keel, which allowed a ship much heavier and larger than a skin boat to be drawn up on a beach, or overland. The keel provided a good setting for a mast and made the hull stronger. It went several inches deeper into the water, preventing the ship from 'making leeway', or being driven sideways by the wind. Speeds of up to 11 knots were possible. The Viking ship could be rowed as well as it could be sailed. It could also be used as a fighting ship, when opponent vessels were lashed together with grappling hooks and the men fought it out with swords. Viking cargo ships had broader and deeper hulls.

With such technology combined with an aggressive spirit, the Norsemen were able to conquer the coast and islands of northern and western Scotland. Their settlement of Scotland was more maritime than in Ireland and England. Apart from Caithness, they rarely penetrated more than a few miles inland and Orkney was a major cross-roads on their routes to Ireland, Iceland, Greenland and America.

As well as islands, the Vikings took control of peninsulas. According to the Orkneyinga Saga, Earl Magnus of Orkney was offered a settlement by the King of the Scots in 1098:

'King Malcolm would let him have all the islands off the west coast which were separated by water navigable by a ship with the rudder set. When King Magnus reached Kintyre he had a skiff hauled across the narrow neck of land at Tarbert, with himself sitting at the helm, and this is how he won the whole peninsula.'

The idea of drawing ships across land was nothing new, for it must have been common with curraghs. The insistence in having the rudder set is more significant, for obviously it was common to unship the side rudder, which would be highly vulnerable when moving over land.

In the middle of the twelfth century Somerled, a chieftain of Norse, Scots and Irish descent, began to create a Hebridean society out of the diverse elements. He defeated the Norsemen with his galley fleet off Islay in 1156 and before his death ten years later he was dealing with the King of Scots. As the mainland kingdom became more powerful, the Norse influence in the west began to decline. The Battle of Largs, in 1263, was not significant in itself. Much more important was the fact that two Viking fleets were destroyed by storms in the Firth of Clyde and forced to retreat to Orkney. By 1266 King Alexander III controlled a realm which approximated to modern Scotland, except that the Northern Isles remained Norwegian until 1468–9 while Berwick was still Scottish.

Sea power in the islands 1263–1500

The Lords of the Isles, descendants of Somerled, created another maritime domain in which the galley was the predominant means of transport and warfare. Carvings of galleys can be seen on West Highland tombstones from about 1350 onwards. They were direct descendants of the Viking ship, though from the fourteenth century they followed north-European practice, adopting the stern rudder instead of the steering oar. Where the rudder is shown it is invariably the modern stern rudder, which must have affected the shape of ships: straight stern posts were used on many galleys, so the ship was no longer double-ended like the Viking ships. The best picture of a galley, on the tomb of Alexander MacLeod of Dunvegan

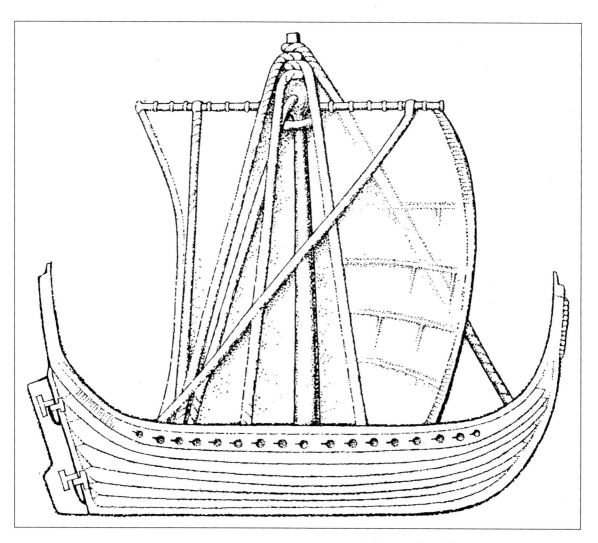

5 The galley carving on the tombstone of Alexander MacLeod of Dunvegan at Rodel, Harris. He died in 1539 but the design of the galley may well look back to an earlier period.

in the church at Rodel, Harris, is dated 1528 and shows many details from Viking times (5). The hull is still clinker-built, with features, such as the design of the bow, which can be seen on the Viking ships found at Roskilde Fjord.

Obviously rowing was essential to the galley and the Rodel boat shows 17 oar ports. According to a document of 1615, a galley proper had 18 to 24 oars (though the Rodel boat was equipped for 34). A birlinn was smaller, with 12 to 18 oars, and a lymphad was probably smaller still.

The Lords of the Isles, chiefs of the Clan Donald, had their headquarters in Finlaggan Castle on Islay. When their supremacy was at its height their domains included all the Western Isles and the Isle of Man, as well as mainland areas in Kintyre, Knapdale and as far east as Badenoch and with the Earldom of Ross to the north. They also held territory in Ireland. As a feudal superior, the Lord of the Isles usually demanded the service of a number of galleys of specified size in return for a holding of land. Thus the Isle of Man was held by Randolph for the service of six galleys of 26 oars and Sleat in Skye was held for a ship of 18 oars. The Lords were subject to the King of

Scots but often showed their independence and dealt on occasion with the kings of Norway and even England.

The Lords too had their internal rivalries. Around 1481 the galleys of John, fourth Lord of the Isles and a 'meek modest man', fought those of his son, Angus Og, in perhaps the biggest sea battle ever fought in Scottish waters, in a bay just north-west of Tobermory. The result was a pyrrhic victory for Angus. The loss of life was great and the site became known as Bloody Bay. In 1498 the title of Lord of the Isles was forfeited to King James IV.

Seaborne trade in the Middle Ages

Eastern Scotland was more peaceful in the eleventh and twelfth centuries. The burgh was central to the concept of trade, for its charter invariably gave its freemen rights to trade in certain areas and commodities. The earliest burghs were founded in the eleventh century and 300, many of them tiny, were established over the years. Before the Railway Age, Scottish trade was almost all maritime. As T C Smout has written of the late seventeenth century, 'Unless you were a packhorse pedlar or a drover, the first essential for carrying on trade was to have or to hire a ship'. A link with the sea was essential for the development of trade, so most burghs were on coasts or navigable rivers and even towns like Stirling are not regarded as especially maritime today.

Berwick became the leading town and port of Scotland, exporting the fine wool produced by the Cistercian monasteries in the Tweed valley. All this ended with the Wars of Independence and in 1296 the town was captured by Edward I of England. It was to change hands 13 times in the next 335 years, but economic development was not compatible with a front-line position.

The east coast was predominant in seaborne trade. Customs accounts of around 1400 show that Ayr, the largest western port, was eighteenth in the list of Scottish burghs. Her trade was valued at £19, compared with £1168 for Edinburgh, £660 for Dundee and £448 for Perth. The Fife ports of Cupar, Inverkeithing, Kinghorn and St Andrews had £334 between them.

The Convention of Royal Burghs, which controlled most of Scotland's trade, established a staple port, through which goods could be exported to Europe. From 1407 it was at Bruges, the greatest port in northern Europe. After 1424 it oscillated between there and Middleburg in Zeeland, and in 1506 it was established in the small but prosperous town of Campveere, or Veere, a few miles to the north (6). A renewal of its lease in 1541 went as follows:

'We grant to these of the said nation, a house within our town of Campveere, the most commodious and convenient that can be found, for those of the said nation, without paying any hire. ... If they are robbed or spoiled of their ships or goods, we shall order restitution at our expense; and likewise we shall cause to be kept buoys and other floating marks, or beacons, in the stream before the said town, to prevent danger or shipwreck.'

The 'Scotch House' at Veere is still there, though the Staple declined in importance and was formally ended in 1847.

Trade, of course, was seasonal and Sir Patrick Spens, for one, was aware of the perils of a winter voyage:

'O wha is this has done this deed,
This ill deed done to me,
To send me out this time of year,
To sail upon the sea.'

Sea power and Scottish independence

The Scottish Wars of Independence began after Alexander III died in 1286 and his young grand-daughter died four years later, leaving the kingdom without a clear heir. The land battles of Stirling Bridge, Falkirk and Bannockburn are commemorated in song, story and film; but in the background, sea power played an essential role. If the English invaded along the east coast, by far the easiest route, they needed ships to keep their army fed,

6 The town of Veere in the Netherlands in 1674.

armed and clothed in a hostile, barren country. If they operated in the west, then supplies and troops from Ireland were essential (7). In the early stages of the wars, Wallace was defeated partly because King Edward of England could keep his sea routes open.

7 Sea power in the English campaigns against Scotland

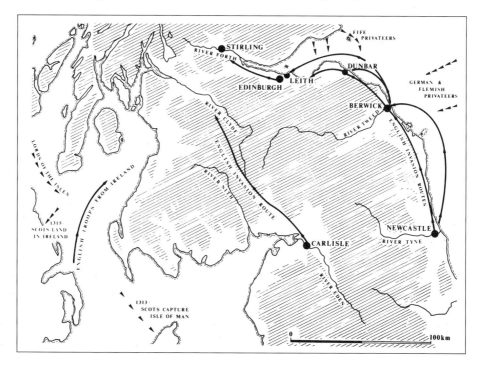

In addition, sea power could do many things for the English in their attempts to conquer Scotland. It allowed an army to cross an estuary such as the Forth, or a sea such as the one dividing Scotland from Ireland. It could besiege coastal fortresses such as Dunbar. It could destroy Scotland's commerce and ruin her trade. As N A M Rodger, the most recent historian of the British Navy, puts it, 'the first essential for English dominance in Scotland remained safe use of the waters on both coasts'. Conversely, the Scots could develop sea power of their own in order to prevent these things and to raid English commerce.

Thus, by 1307, King Robert Bruce's alliance with the Western Islanders gave him the use of galleys to harass English shipping and from 1310 he had the assistance of Flemish and German privateers. His forces captured the Isle of Man in 1313 and interrupted English communication with Ireland for a year. In 1315 Bruce's brother landed in Ireland with 6000 men transported in 300 ships and for a time they dominated the Irish Sea. In the meantime, the English merchants were becoming tired of the king's constant requisitioning of their ships and the interruption of trade and became less enthusiastic for the war.

The Auld Alliance between Scotland and France began in 1295 and was strengthened in 1326, when Robert the Bruce agreed to the Treaty of Corbell with the French king. This was only possible because of the sea links between the two countries, despite the commanding position of England between the two.

The alliance led to links between the two royal families and sometimes to disaster. Thus, in 1406, the 12-year-old Prince James, soon to be James I, was sent to France for his safety and education. Off Flamborough Head in Yorkshire his ship, the *Maryenknyght of Hamburg*, was captured by the English pirate Hughe-atte Fen, and he spent the next 18 years imprisoned in England, until he was ransomed for £40,000.

It was a civil war which led to the rise of the first Scottish naval hero, Sir Andrew Wood

of Largo. James III, faced with a revolt of lowland nobles nominally led by his own son, got out of a tight corner by using Wood's ships to escape to Fife. When the rebels were nevertheless successful and James IV was crowned as king in 1488, Wood accepted the new regime and fought against the English. In August 1490, in his famous ship the *Yellow Carvel*, he defeated three English vessels under Stephen Bull off the Isle of May and towed them into Dundee in triumph.

James IV's navy

James IV built a fleet of galleys based at Dumbarton and used them to suppress the Lords of the Isles. He built a very different navy in the Firth of Forth. Like other kings of the age he bought, hired and requisitioned merchant ships for his fleet and he issued private men-of-war, or privateers, with 'letters of marque' which allowed them to make war on the king's enemies. The best known captains of the reign, apart from Andrew Wood, were John, Andrew and Robert Barton of Leith, whose campaigns often strayed into piracy.

But a real 'Navy Royal' needed larger ships, which the king had to build for himself. More aware of developments in Europe than any other Scottish king, he knew that converted merchant ships were less useful than in the past, for a new and larger type had evolved – the carrack – which had high castles and an armament of numerous but light guns to fire down on an enemy's decks. The only Scottish king to build a navy for more than home defence, he perhaps intended it to become a factor in European politics, to support his allies in France or Denmark. Perhaps he felt that such a fleet was an essential part of the 'new monarchy' which he represented. His first 'great ship', the *Margarret*, was launched at Leith in 1505. She was of perhaps 600 or 700 tons with four masts and similar to the English *Mary Rose* of four years later.

James was dissatisfied with the shallow water of Leith and built Newhaven a mile further up the River Forth. However, this was still

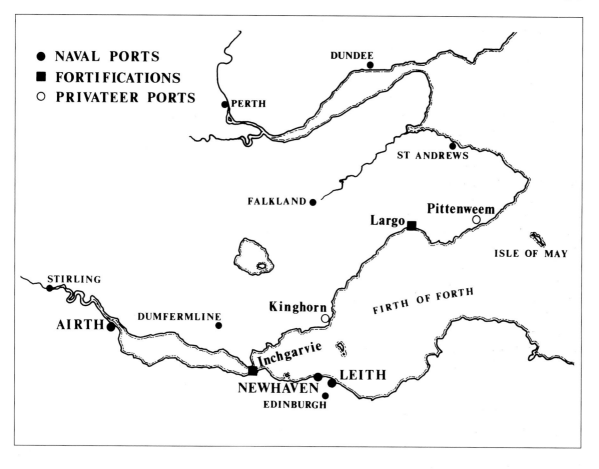

8 Naval bases and other ports in the Firth of Forth in the time of James IV.

exposed to attack and he started another dock-yard at the Pool of Airth, on the south bank of the Forth just above the modern Kincardine Bridge. It was in use by 1506 (8).

By this time James had already conceived the most famous of all his maritime projects – the *Great Michael*, arguably the first modern warship. Her building at Newhaven took five years. The chronicler Pitscottie claims, with no exaggeration, that she 'tuik so mekill timber that scho wastit all the wodis in Fyfe except Falkland wode, by (besides) all the tymmer that was gottin out of Noroway'. Shipwrights were brought in from France to supervise the work and the ship cost the enormous sum of £30,000 Scots. She was launched in October 1511 to a fanfare of trumpets.

The ship, according to Pitscottie, was 240 ft (73 m) long and 35 ft (10.7 m) broad, with sides 10 ft (3 m) thick (9). This makes no sense in terms of contemporary ship design unless perhaps Pitscottie was using the length overall, including the bowsprit and other rigging and the two sides combined were 10 ft thick, or 5 ft each. Perhaps a more likely figure would be a hull of 180 ft (55 m) on the main deck, with a keel of about 120 ft (36.6 m) and a breadth of 45 ft (13.7 m), giving a ship of about 1200 tons. Oddly enough, her hull shape is marked out near the remains of Tullibardine Castle near Auchterarder and an accurate measure-ment of that would probably reveal her true size. In any case, she was far bigger than any other ship in Scotland, and any built in the fol-lowing three centuries. The French ambassador, entertained on board her in February 1513, wrote that she was 'so powerful that another

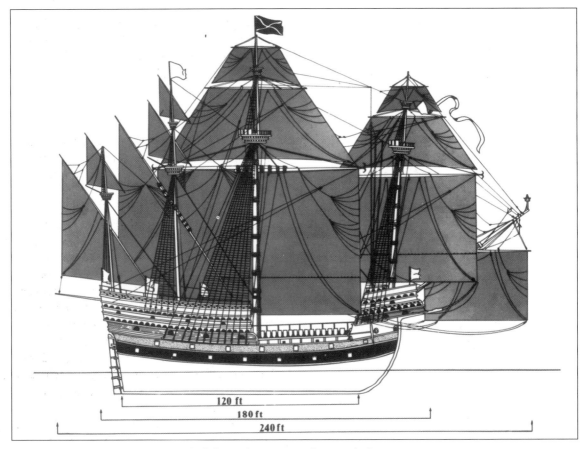

120 ft

180 ft

240 ft

9 A possible reconstruction of the *Great Michael*, showing how Pitscottie's figures might fit.

10 A French galley of the time of John Knox.

such would not be found in Christendom'. Henry VIII of England, never one to be out-done by his poor relation to the north, launched a slightly bigger ship, the *Great Harry*, three years later.

James's great fleet was barely used. The king was killed at the Battle of Flodden and the regency which succeeded him had no interest in sea power. *The Great Michael* was sold to France and may have served for another 30 years.

Sea power in the age of reformation

When the German Reformation began in 1520 with the publication of Martin Luther's Tracts, the ideas for new church organization and the-ology soon spread to Scotland through the trading links of the east coast ports. When the Crown and the Church repressed these ideas, reformers such as George Wishart and John Knox crossed the seas to find refuge in Germany or Geneva, where their ideas were considerably reinforced.

Opposition to the Reformation came from the Scottish Crown's traditional ally, France. In May 1546, local Protestant lairds captured St Andrews Castle and hung the body of Cardinal Beaton from a window. Royal forces besieged the castle for more than a year until 17 French galleys came to their aid (10). They brought four 'cannons royal', which would have needed teams of 32 oxen each had they been moved by land. Guns from Scottish castles were brought by boat and set up on St Salvator's Church and the Cathedral, joining two Scottish guns, 'cruik mow and deaff Neg'. The bombardment was so devastating that the castle surrendered with-in three hours. John Knox and many other Protestants then had another taste of French sea power, being forced to spend two years as galley slaves.

When Philip of Spain sent his Armada against England in 1588, he was partly inspired by the execution of the Roman Catholic Mary Queen of Scots by Elizabeth of England. By this time the lowland Scots were firmly Protestant, and the country maintained a pro-English neutrality as the Armada fled round its coastline after being dispersed by the English. Crews from Spanish ships which were wrecked in the islands met with a mixed recep-tion. The Catholic islanders had a natural sym-pathy and sometimes helped them to escape; this was combined with a tendency to loot the wealthy Spaniards. The *San Juan de Sicilia* put into Tobermory Bay and was blown up, proba-bly an act of sabotage by a lowland Scot.

Seventeenth-century trade

In 1603 James VI of Scotland inherited the English throne as James I, but Scotland and England retained their separate parliaments and governments. James ruled from London and was much influenced by English affairs, so Scottish traders had a bad deal. One of the first complaints was about the new Union Flag itself, because the 'Scottis Croce, called Sanctandrous Croce, is twyse divydit, and the Inglishe Croce, callit Sanct George, haldin haill and drawne through the Scottis Croce, whiche is thairby obscurit'.

James used his control of Scotland, England and Ireland to drive a wedge between the potential Catholic rebels of Ulster and the Hebrides. From 1608 he settled many Scottish Protestants in the province of Ulster, the least anglicized area of the island until then.

Scottish trade benefited from a relatively stable environment until the outbreak of the English Civil War in 1642, but her merchants were increasingly cut out of the developing trade between England and her colonies in the West Indies and North America. The English Parliament first passed the Navigation Act in 1651, decreeing that English and colonial trade could only be carried in English ships. Within a year Scotland was united with England after conquest by Oliver Cromwell, so the Act had no great effect. But after the restoration of the Stewart dynasty in the person of Charles II in 1660, a new English Navigation Act was passed, much to the disadvantage of the Scots. They retaliated with their own Act, but Scottish trade was a tiny fraction of that of

England, so it was no threat to the English.

Even in peacetime, there were many dangers to Scottish trade. In 1618 John Stewart a 'vagabond' and Margaret Barclay, the wife of a burgess of Irvine, were tried for witchcraft in connection with 'the drowning and perisheing of the schip callit the *Gift of God*'. Stewart hanged himself and Margaret Barclay was executed.

Seamen captured by Barbary corsairs from the north coast of Africa, unless they were ransomed, might face a life of 'great slaverie and miserie and subject to all the contumeleis that these miserable miscreants can inflict upon thame'. In 1624, for example, the government appealed for 2,400 merks to rescue one John Murray, asking the ministers of the church to 'steir up thair flokes to schaw and extend thair cherrites and benevolence'.

The Western Isles could be dangerous too, because of the people as well as the navigational hazards. In 1627 the ship *Providence of Dumbartane* was wrecked on Mull and looted by the McLeans of Duart, who took 'fyftein lasts of herring or thairby at two hundred merkes, extending to thrie thowsand merkes, two thowsand weight of Yreland butter, woth sevin hundreth merkes, mair of cloath and uther small wairis worth fyve hundreth merkes'.

Despite all the handicaps, Scottish trade grew during the seventeenth century. Most of the exports were still the produce of an undeveloped country – wool, hides, herring and salmon. The coal industry was just beginning to grow and its products created a greater need for shipping volume, for both coastal trade and export.

Despite English prohibition, Scottish trade with the American and West Indian colonies was also growing and partly as a result, Glasgow rose in importance. The city paid 4 per cent of the Scottish tax roll in 1612 and 20 per cent in 1705. Scottish ships were still tiny, averaging about 50 tons and rarely more than 70 tons. By the end of the century, perhaps 200 sea-going ships were flying the Scottish flag.

They had mostly been built in England or the Netherlands. Scotland's harbours were small, apart from the new one at Port Glasgow, started in 1668, but it was widely recognized that a thriving foreign trade could lift Scotland beyond a subsistence economy, constantly threatened with famine when crops failed.

Naval power in the seventeenth century

In 1650, following the Royalist defeat in the English Civil War and the execution of his father, the young Charles II sailed for Scotland from Holland, landing at Speymouth. To crush him, Oliver Cromwell invaded Scotland in traditional fashion, using his navy to support the army in its march up the east coast. Victorious at Dunbar, Cromwell used ships to remove treasure and public records from Scotland and to control the islands.

After the Union of the Crowns of 1603 and even more so under the Cromwellian conquest, Scottish foreign policy was subjected to the needs of the English. Between 1652 and 1674, three 'Anglo-Dutch' wars were fought and all were extremely unpopular in Scotland, because most of the country's trade still passed through the Staple at Veere. The Scots had no navy to protect their own trade, but were obliged to raise men for the Royal Navy (11). At the outbreak of the second war in 1664, for example, they were ordered to provide 500 seamen, but many of the men liable to be pressed fled the country and embargoes on shipping and the threat of fines were needed to raise the levy. Privateering was far more popular and Scottish captains were able to raid the rich commerce of the Dutch.

In 1689 the Roman Catholic King James VII of Scotland was deposed by William of Orange. For more than half a century after that James's supporters, the Jacobites, aimed to have him or his son restored to the throne. They were especially strong in the Highlands of Scotland, where the inhabitants were unhappy about the settlement after the Revolution of 1689 and the central government's attempts to control them, represented most brutally by the

11 Fort Charlotte in Lerwick was built in 1665 to defend the harbour during the Second Anglo-Dutch War. It was burnt by the Dutch in 1673 and rebuilt in 1782, during yet another war with the Dutch.

Massacre of Glencoe in 1692.

Because of a war with France, the Scottish Navy was revived in 1688/9, when Parliament ordered 'two frigates to be provided to cruise on the west coast of this kingdom'. These were tiny hired ships from Glasgow. They were soon captured by three French men of war in the North Channel. One was recaptured by the English and ignominiously sunk as a breakwater in their dockyard at Sheerness.

An east coast force was founded in 1694 to assist English warships against Jacobites on the Bass Rock in the Firth of Forth. In 1695 the Parliamentary Committee of Trade was of the opinion 'that a naval force is absolutely necessary for the encouraging and security of the trade and defending of our coasts', especially in view of the menace posed by French privateers. Three men of war, of 20 to 32 guns each, were ordered from shipyards on the River Thames and commissioned in 1696. In 1707 they were merged into the English fleet and the last Scottish Navy became extinct.

The Darien scheme

Excluded from the English colonies, the Scots decided to set up an enterprise of their own to get some share of the enormous profits which the English were making in the West Indies, North America and India. Money was raised from small and large investors all over Scotland and in London, largely by William Paterson who founded the Bank of England, but the English investors were forced to withdraw because of pressure from the English East India Company.

The 'Company of Scotland Trading to Africa and the Indies' was not at first committed to any specific area. Since Scotland had no

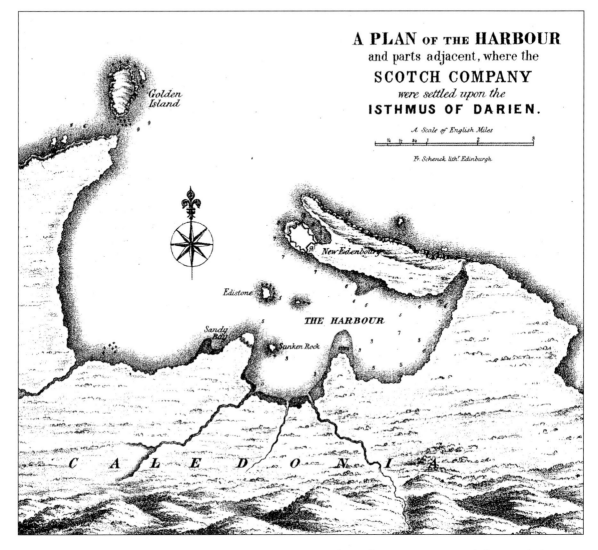

12 The Scottish settlement at Darien, showing the fort at New Edinburgh.

yard capable of building ocean-going ships, agents were sent abroad to purchase them – an Englishman at Hamburg reported, 'We have here at present a certaine crew of Scotchmen sent hither from ye East India Companie of Scotland to buy and build ships for ye trade'. At Amsterdam they contracted for a ship with a keel 134 ft (40.8 m) long, built 'of good Forin oak all the beams lett doun in the Clamps with good Dovetaills'.

In July 1698 five ships sailed from Leith, carrying the hopes of the nation with them. Off Madeira the captains opened their sealed orders to 'proceed to the Bay of Darien and make the isle called the Golden Island ... and there make a settlement on the mainland as well as the said island, if proper (as we believe) and unpossessed by an European nation'. Arriving there in November, the sailors perceived the harbour to be 'a most excellent one'. Fort St Andrew and New Edinburgh were established, but soon the colonists were skirmishing with the Spanish and falling prey to dysentery and fever (12). King William refused any help to the Scottish colonists, because he did not want to offend his Spanish allies. The attempt was abandoned but only the flagship, the *Caledonia*, completed the journey home.

A second expedition left from Greenock in May 1699, unaware that the colony had been given up. They arrived in November, but in March 1700 they had to surrender to the Spanish. The whole Darien Scheme had cost Scotland several hundred lives and about £200,000 of her very limited capital.

The Scottish colonists have been much criticized for their naivety, for taking goods such as Bibles and wigs to trade with the Indians, but they were no worse than the first English colonists in North America, a century earlier. The Jamestown settlement in Virginia, for example, barely survived its first few years, and the Scottish problems were due to inexperience rather than foolishness.

Relations between Scotland and England worsened after a Scottish ship was impounded off Kent in 1704. Soon afterwards the

English East Indiaman *Worcester* put into Leith, having sailed round the north of Scotland to avoid French privateers. The crew, under Captain Green, were convicted of piracy against a missing Darien Company ship, the inaptly named *Speedy Return*, which in fact had sunk in the Indian Ocean. Watched by a crowd of 80,000 Scots, Green and two of his crew were hanged on Leith Sands, dying 'with invincible patience, like innocent men'.

Things were now so bad that complete severance between Scotland and England seemed possible: but the Scots were offered full free trade with the English empire and eventually on the 1 May 1707, the two Parliaments and governments were united. It has been described as 'a political necessity for England, a commercial necessity for Scotland'.

13 The Jacobite campaigns, 1708–1746.

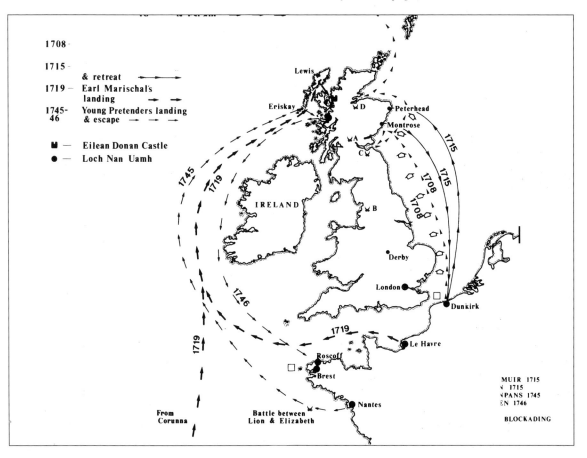

14 After his landing on the Scottish mainland at Loch Nan Uamh, Prince Charles takes his leave of Antoine Walsh, who had provided the ship for the passage.

Naval power and the Jacobites

Despite the Union of the Parliaments, the Highlands of Scotland were not part of the British nation in any real sense. Cultural and economic differences were reinforced by the fact that most of the Highlanders remained supporters of the Jacobites, while the rest of the United Kingdom, including lowland Scotland, was generally satisfied with the prosperity it found under the Hanoverian regime, established in 1714. The Jacobites came to rely increasingly on support from France. It was sea communication, or lack of it, which determined the course of the various rebellions. Its importance is hinted at in the song 'Over the Sea to Skye' and in the Jacobite toast 'The King over the Water'.

In 1708 James Stewart, the Pretender, hoping to exploit disgruntlement with the Union, sailed from Dunkirk with 6000 French troops in almost 30 ships (13). He was closely pursued by the English Admiral Byng, failed to land in the Firth of Forth and retreated round the north of Scotland. In 1715, after the unattractive George I became king, the Earl of Mar raised the standard of revolt at Braemar, but was already defeated before the Pretender himself could reach Scotland at the end of the year. In 1719 a party of Jacobites led by Lord Tullibardine and Earl Marischal, with the support of the Spanish government, landed in the west and held Eilean Donan Castle with a few troops, until it was recaptured by British naval forces and the main Jacobite force was defeated a few miles away at Glenshiel.

The most famous rising, of course, began in 1745 and was led by the Pretender's son, Prince Charles Edward Stewart. He had hoped for a large-scale invasion of southern England in 1744, but the French fleet was dispersed by storms. Undeterred, he sailed from Nantes in the small frigate *le Du Teillay*. Her consort, the *Elisabeth*, was captured after an epic fight with the British ship *Lion*, but the Prince succeeded in landing at Moidart with his famous 'seven men' and raised the standard at Glenfinnan (14). French convoys, however, failed to reach him because of bad weather or British blockade, contributing to the Jacobite isolation. After his defeat at Culloden in 1746, Prince Charles went into hiding and the French made six separate attempts to rescue him, one of which led to a small naval battle in Loch man Uamh, before he was eventually taken back to Roscoff in Britanny in the frigate *Heureux*.

It was in the second half of the eighteenth century, after the Highlands had been brought under control, however brutally, after full economic union between Scotland and England, after trade had developed between Scotland and America, and after peace and stability were established in the country, that the modern phase in Scotland's maritime history began. From being a remote country on the edge of Europe, constantly in fear of invasion from Romans, Vikings or English, Scotland was about to enter the world stage as a centre of trade, industry, shipbuilding and maritime power.

2
Trade and Transport

Ferries in the east

Sea transport did two things for Scotland: it held the country together by a system of ferries, without which it would never have existed as a nation: and it provided the only means of communication with the outside world except with England. Without sea transport, the country would have been poor and totally dependent on England for economic and cultural progress.

Sea transport was all the more necessary because roads were bad. As Thomas Morer wrote in 1689, 'Stage coaches they have none. ... The truth is, the roads will hardly allow 'em these conveniences'. It was 1749 before a regular coach service was set up between Glasgow and Edinburgh and even that took 12 hours.

The Firth of Forth almost divides Scotland in two. Its most famous crossing was at Queensferry, where the Firth narrows to a mile and a quarter. Named after the landing place of Queen Margaret in 1071, it was a public service, dating from a grant in 1129, free to pilgrims on the way to St Andrews. Daniel Defoe described another route from Leith to Burntisland in 1724, 'As 'tis no less than seven

15 A primitive ferry, used to punt horses and people across the River Tweed at Kelso, portrayed by John Slezer, c 1680

miles, and that sometimes they meet with bad weather, the passengers are so often frighted that I knew several gentlemen that would always choose to go round the Queensferry'. In addition, there were ferries between North Berwick and Elie, and shorter crossings of the Forth at Kincardine and Alloa (15).

Proceeding north, a traveller would cross the River Tay from Ferryport on Craig (now Newport) to Dundee. The ferry was important enough for rates to be fixed by Parliament in 1551, 'For ilk man and horse, eight pennies, and for ilk man or woman be themselves, four pennies'. According to Robert Stevenson in the 1820s, it was operated by 30 boats and 50 men. During fogs ferrymen, too poor to afford compasses, dropped straw over the stern to ascertain the direction of the current.

Further north, there was a ferry at Montrose and in 1673 there was a complaint that the ferry at Montrose stopped on Sunday, by order of the Minister. At Aberdeen, the ferry across the Dee was set up by Sir John Forbes in 1679. For crossing the Cromarty Firth, the main route was Nigg to Cromarty.

Ferries in the west

Ferries on the River Clyde held the region together rather than serving travellers passing through. Downstream of Glasgow Bridge, the Govan ferry was of some antiquity (colour plate 1): in 1785 Glasgow Town Council agreed, 'there has always been a public road from the Broomielaw to the Govan ferry'. There was another between Yoker and Renfrew, the 'east ferry' at Erskine and the 'west ferry' near Dumbarton, with the 'long ferry' between Cardross and Newark (later Port Glasgow). In the earliest days these ferries were simple rowing boats, but flat vessels capable of carrying carts were used on the shorter routes by the nineteenth century. In 1857 the Govan Ferry used an ingenious system with a chain across the river, on which the boat was hauled by a cog operated by the crew.

In their *Tour to the Hebrides* in 1773,

Samuel Johnson and James Boswell used the private transport of the clan chiefs for longer voyages. Boswell described his trip in the Laird of Raasay's boat, a descendant of the Lords of the Isles' galleys:

'We had four stout rowers, particularly a Macleod. Mr Johnson sat high on the head like a magnificent Triton. Malcolm raised an Erse [ie Gaelic] song, *'Haytin foam foam eri'*, to which he gave Jacobite words of his own. The boatmen and Mr Macqueen chorused, and all went well. At length Malcolm took an oar and rowed like a hero.'

For shorter voyages, they used regular ferries. Between Mull and Ulva they failed to hail one over a 200 yard strait, because the night was too dark and the wind too strong. One from Lochbuie in Mull to Oban had the bottom 'strewed with branches of trees or bushes, upon which we sat'. Vehicle and horse ferries were unknown, because of the rarity of wheeled transport.

There were also ferries across the sea-lochs. Otter Ferry, crossing Loch Fyne between Mid-Argyll and Cowal, was improved in 1773 when the road from Dunoon was re-aligned by the Commissioners of Supply and a small jetty and ferry house were built at East Otter.

The most important Highland trade was in cattle, and beasts from the islands often used the most primitive form of sea transport imaginable. When crossing narrow straits, such as Kyle Rhea between Skye and the mainland, the cattle were tied together head to tail in groups of six or eight and forced to swim, led by men in a boat. In slightly longer passages, for example between Jura and Knapdale, they were put into a vessel 'of great width of beam, and the cattle were fastened with their heads to rings on the gunwale on each side'.

Glasgow and the tobacco trade

In 1598 an English traveller wrote, 'Since the Scots are very daring, I cannot see why their Marriners should not bee bold and courageous, howsoever they have not hitherto made any long voyages, rather for want of riches, than

16 The port of Greenock in 1768, with ships at anchor and the harbour crowded with shipping. Scottish artists had not yet learned to make realistic drawings of ships.

for slothfulness or want of courage'. From 1668, when a ship from Dumbarton was the first from Scotland to find her way across the Atlantic, this began to change. The Union of 1707 legalized trade with America and the Scots were soon ready to take advantage of it. The Scottish trade was run by a small group of Glasgow merchants known as the Tobacco Lords who controlled about 30 per cent of British tobacco imports by the 1770s. English merchants attributed this success to customs fraud, which led to an enquiry in 1722–3. More likely, the Tobacco Lords were successful because they established a tight system of credit with the planters of Virginia, setting up warehouses to store the tobacco until ready for export.

Glasgow also had geographical advantages. In wartime (more than half the eighteenth century) the Clyde was a long way from enemy activity in the English Channel. Most of the tobacco was taken by road and later canal across the narrowest neck of Britain to the Forth and re-exported to northern Europe. Trade with France, the biggest peacetime market for re-exported tobacco, peaked at over £500,000 in 1773. Ships in the tobacco trade took out manufactured goods to sell to the Americans. Scottish industry could not supply enough at the beginning of the eighteenth century, so goods were imported from England and then re-exported: this provided a stimulus and an example for Scotland to develop industries of her own.

As Scottish shipbuilding was primitive, the Tobacco Lords chartered ships from English ports such as Whitehaven or had them built in America, where timber was plentiful. Tobacco was carried in casks known as hogsheads, 3 ft (0.9 m) long and 2 ft 3 in (0.6 m) in diameter, which was the measure of size of a ship in the trade; thus in 1775 the American agent of W Cunninghame & Co 'chartered the *Lonsdale of Whitehaven*, James Gray, master, of 430 hogsheads burthen'. Since four hogsheads were equivalent to a ton, the ship was just over 100 tons by normal measurement – perhaps 60 ft (18.3 m) long and 20 ft (6 m) broad in the hull, smaller than a Clyde puffer.

In 1763–66 there were 18 Glasgow vessels trading with Virginia, compared with 90 from London, 53 from Bristol, 13 from Whitehaven and six from Liverpool. Of those from Glasgow, 12 were ships, three-masted with square sails on each mast, two were snows and two were brigs, with two masts. All were standard merchantmen of the age. The hulls tended to be broad at the waterline and narrower above ('tumble-home'). The bows were bluff, the stern surmounted with a large, square cabin with windows for the comfort of officers and passengers.

By 1775, when the American colonists began their revolt against the British, the Scots were unpopular in Virginia and found it difficult to get cargoes. Because of American privateers, fast, well-armed ships were now at an advantage: one was advertised for sale in 1780, 'The *Aeolus* sails well, has six carriage guns'. Others had to go in convoy, which reduced them to the speed of the slowest ship. The War of American Independence came into Scottish waters in 1778–9 when John Paul Jones, born in Kirkcudbrightshire and now a citizen of Virginia, caused panic with his privateers *Ranger* and *Bonnehomme Richard*. The fort at Lerwick in Shetland was rebuilt at this time, and given the name Fort Charlotte.

The Scottish tobacco trade never recovered from the war. Debts were never repaid; the former colonies, the United States from 1787, were not bound by the Navigation Laws and could trade with whomever they pleased. Many of the Tobacco Lords moved into other businesses, while the Scots had developed an overseas trade far greater than ever before and Scottish industry was beginning to develop.

The Industrial Revolution and shipping

All three industries which drove the Industrial Revolution in Scotland depended heavily on sea transport. The cotton industry relied on raw materials from America and on overseas markets in Europe, the Empire and America. The iron industry was led by the Carron Ironworks, founded in 1759. Its most famous product, the carronade, was a light gun of large bore, used by naval and merchant ships in the wars with France up to 1815. The company operated its own fleet of ships from 1786. The coal industry, which expanded about five-fold in the eighteenth century, was the greatest user of shipping because of the volume of its products. Since there was no other way of moving bulk cargoes over any distance, the

essential slowness and unpredictability of sail was tolerated. In 1807 James Primrose of Kincardine, master of the *Peggy and Nelly* of 60 tons, recorded that a voyage from his home port to Dundee and Perth might take five and a half days in good conditions, three weeks in bad – a journey of less than 100 miles by sea and 25 by land.

A typical merchant ship is described in the Greenock register, instituted by law in 1786. The *Jeannie* of Port Glasgow was:

'*British* built, has *one* deck and *two* masts; that her length, from the Fore-part of the Main Stem to the After-part of the Stern post aloft, is *eighty* Feet and *ten* inches [24.6 m]; her Breadth at the broadest Part, being above the Main Wales, *twenty-three* feet and *eight* inches [7.6 m]; her depth *fifteen* feet and *two* inches [4.6 m]; and admeasures *one hundred and seventy-eight* tons: that she is a *square sterned, full Built brigantine, with a break in her Deck*, has *no* gallery and *a serpent* head.'

Registered in 1796, she was owned by seven partners in Port Glasgow and Glasgow. Intended for the West India trade, she had a crew of 13 men and carried four 4-pounder guns for defence.

Scotland had a slowly growing import trade in food from Holland, though the export trade never fully recovered from the loss of America: it was almost eliminated during wars in 1780–3 and from 1795. Ireland provided a steady market, largely immune to the effects of war. Across the Atlantic, the West Indies partly replaced the now independent colonies, while trade with Canada was significant by the end of the century. Imports and exports from the former colonies also rose, as much with northern states like New York as with Virginia.

Scottish shipping increased through the late eighteenth century. Including coasting and foreign trades, there were 1567 ships totalling 92,000 tons in 1772. In 1822, as the steam age began to dawn in Scotland, there were 3071 ships totalling 277,000 tons.

Ferries in the steam age

The railway age, which began about 1830 in Scotland, was a boost to shipping in its early stages, rather than a rival. Railway engines consumed large amounts of coal, which was mainly moved by sea. Railways greatly increased the demand for passenger transport and developed public taste for travel. Ships provided a means of connecting directly with scheduled train services. The most famous travel guide of the period, usually associated with railways, was *Bradshaw's General Railway and Steam Navigation Guide* and listed all passenger services within Britain and to Europe.

The first train ferries were set up on the Forth in 1850 and the Tay three years later. The first, the *Leviathan*, was double-ended with two railway tracks and operated from Granton to Burntisland, using a form of 'link span' which later became vital in allowing car ferries to load at any state of the tide (17). The *Leviathan* carried loaded waggons without their engine, not complete trains with passengers. The first Tay Rail Bridge was built in 1878 but collapsed disastrously the following year, bringing the ferry back into operation. The new Tay Bridge opened in 1887 and the Forth Bridge in 1890. However, there was still a demand for passenger and vehicle services over the estuaries, growing with the advance of the motor vehicle until they were stopped abruptly by the building of road bridges in the 1960s.

Rowing ferries were dangerous in the increasingly crowded waters of Glasgow Harbour; 19 people were lost when one capsized in 1864, causing the Clyde Trustees to introduce their first steam ferry the following year. It was double-ended with an innovative water-jet on each quarter. It proved uneconomic and another boat was built in 1867, with a similar hull but conventional propellers. At the same time, the Trustees introduced a new vehicle ferry at Govan, still on a chain but now powered by steam and able to carry two or three carts with their horses. In 1890 the Trustees built the *Finnieston*, double ended with four screws and an elevating vehicle deck so that it could be used at any height of tide without a ramp, which took up a valuable space in a crowded city. Similar boats were introduced at Whiteinch in 1905 and Govan in 1912.

In 1884, 500 horse-drawn buses took passengers between Glasgow and Whiteinch and Govan. Four ferries, the *Cluthas*, were built to take on some of this task and eight more in the next eight years. They carried nearly 3 million passengers in their peak year, linking the city centre with the shipyards and docks downstream. *Clutha No 9*, built in 1891, could carry 360 cramped passengers on a 74 ft (22.5 m) hull. In the late nineteenth century, Glasgow became a truly maritime city, with many of her population working in docks, shipyards and

17 The 'floating railway' from Granton to Burntisland, which began in 1850 and was the first train ferry in the world.

shipping offices, transported to work across or along the River Clyde and taking their recreation on Clyde steamers. The situation did not last far into the twentieth century, for an electric tramway opened in 1903 and the *Cluthas* were withdrawn.

At Renfrew and Erskine, downriver from Glasgow, were steam-powered chain ferries which could carry vehicles. In such rural locations, there was no problem with a long fixed ramp and the double-ended ferries had their own ramps which were lowered on approaching the shore. Most of them closed in the 1960s, when the Clyde Tunnel opened, followed by high level road bridges at Erskine and Kingston, Glasgow. The Renfrew Ferry survives in reduced form.

The coasting trades

From around 1700, ships operated a regular service between Leith and London, but passengers often preferred the faster salmon smacks operating out of Berwick. In 1791 the Leith and London Shipping Company began a regular smack service from Leith. In 1801, 19 vessels sailed the route, with crews of 18 or 19 men. Steam began with the *United Kingdom* in 1826 and in 1831 the Steamboat Companion referred to 'the convenient and elegant accommodation now afforded by the numerous steam vessels on the east coast', which had 'induced the majority of those who visit Scotland to prefer this mode of travelling to the more fatiguing conveyance by coach'. In 1841 the London and Edinburgh Shipping Company introduced 'Aberdeen clippers' to give a faster passage under sail, but in the following decade it too turned to steam, against railway competition. By 1877 there were seven ships a week between the Forth and Thames, including Carron steamers 'specially built for this service ... fitted up with all modern improvements ... lighted throughout with electricity'. Even in 1939, six ships a week maintained a regular service for passengers and cargo.

On the Clyde and elsewhere, local goods transport was by small sailing barges called gabbarts. The details of the type are obscure; there are no surviving examples, no plans and very few pictures. From about 1631 the Town Council of Dumbarton employed a 'cobar' of about 10 tons for loading ships in the port with cargoes of salt and coal. If we can believe the drawings in Slezer's *Theatrum Scotiae* of 1693 (and they seem to be fairly accurate in their depiction of ships), small craft in the Clyde had a single, one-piece mast with a yard set diagonally, perhaps carrying a form of lug-sail. One appears on the early Greenock shipping register, described as of one deck, one mast, 30 tons: perhaps others were too small to qualify. By about 1800, most pictures of the Clyde show small craft which are gaff-cutter rigged. Some pictures show a strong curve or sheer on the hull, with a high, pointed stern perhaps and lee-boards to prevent it from being driven sideways in the wind. Others show a very flat hull. Photographs of the *Princess Mayse* of 1893, on the other hand,

18 The gabbart *Mary* in the Holy Loch in the 1880s. Probably built in 1845 at Bowling, this vessel is very similar to a Mersey flat.

show a very square stern and a moderate amount of sheer. The *Mary* of Glasgow, built in 1845, seems to have had a very low freeboard, while the *Margaret Dewar* of 1874 had higher sides (18). Probably the gabbart was not a specific type, but a generic term for small estuary and river cargo craft.

The gabbart's disappearance might be explained by the rapid progress of steam on the Clyde, which left the sailing craft as a despised poor relation. Neil Munro's fictional skipper Para Handy often compares his puffer *Vital Spark* to 'a common gaabert'.

19 The evolution of the puffer:

a) (top) *Steam Lighter no 9* , built in 1871 for the Carron Iron Company by Barclay Curle, is an example of the early type of 'inside' boat.

b) (middle) The *Garmoyle* and *Ailsa*, built by Denny of Dumbarton in a rare venture into the coasting trade in 1908, were 66 ft 6 in long to pass through the locks of the Forth and Clyde Canal.

c) (bottom) The *Moonlight* of 1952 was a diesel-powered puffer, 88 ft long, for the Crinan Canal.

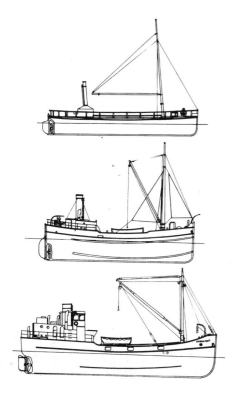

The puffer

The Clyde puffer was essentially a small coaster, as beloved locally as the barges of the Thames estuary or the schooners of Maine. While other nations commemorate their past with sailing craft, it is perhaps appropriate that the Scots, the pioneers of steam, should esteem a vessel which is short, smoky and not conventionally pretty. Part of the reason, of course, is the Para Handy tales of Neil Munro, which have inspired two television series. But real-life puffermen have tended to resent the carefree, irresponsible but lovable image created by fiction.

The type originated with the *Thomas* of 1856, an iron canal boat with a simple steam engine without a condenser, so that it 'puffed' with every stroke. She had bluff bows to carry the maximum cargo and was less than 66 ft (20 m) long, to fit into the locks of the canal. By the 1870s, the design was being adapted for use outside the canal. Bulwarks were added to keep the deck dry: the engine, which had relied on fresh canal water, was replaced by a more conventional one with a condenser. A derrick was added for cargo handling and the classic puffer was born – already a misnomer, as the characteristic puffing stroke no longer happened.

Three different types developed (19). The 'inside' boats remained on the Forth and Clyde. 'Shorehead' boats operated within the Firth of Clyde above Bute and in Loch Fyne, but were still 66 ft (20 m) long. Both types had a crew of three. The 'outside' boat was designed for the far more challenging waters of the Hebrides. It had a crew of four and was 88 ft (26.8 m) long, the size of locks in the Crinan Canal across the Kintyre peninsula.

The outside puffer was supremely adaptable. Its engineer needed little training. It could unload on a beach at low water, using its own derrick. Its crew accommodation was adequate for several days away from home. The skipper had a small cabin in the stern, while the mate, engineer and deckhand lived in the forecastle, with a table and a cooking stove. The steering wheel replaced the tiller in the 1870s, and in the twentieth century a deckhouse was built over it.

The main trade of the outside boats was with the islands. They carried coal and manufactures out from the docks of Glasgow or Bowling, but often had to return empty or partly loaded, unless they could find seaweed for iodine or whisky from Islay. During the month of March 1880 the *Starlight*, an inside boat belonging to Ross and Marshall, carried furniture from Greenock to Kilcreggan, coal from Glasgow to Ayr, Greenock to Girvan and to the Holy Loch. She spent 24 days working and seven, including Sundays, idle.

About 400 puffers were built over the years and operated by more than 50 companies. There were more than 20 builders in Scotland, mostly on the Forth and Clyde Canal at Kirkintilloch and at Maryhill, though bigger yards built them on occasion. The first to be fitted with an internal combustion engine was the *Innisgara* of 1912, but strangely, the steam-powered puffer was revived by its usefulness in servicing ships of war. Having used them at Scapa Flow in 1914-8, in 1939 the Royal Navy ordered a new class of steamships, the VICs, mostly from English yards (20). Some were bought into the trade after 1945, though diesel became common in new vessels. In 1975–7 new ships, too large for the Crinan Canal, were bought by Hay-Hamilton to keep up the trade against competition from road and ferry. When government subsidies were abolished in 1993, the last operator, Glenlight Shipping Ltd, withdrew.

The Clyde steamer

Henry Bell began his pioneering steamboat service between Glasgow and his hotel in Helensburgh in the *Comet* in 1812, setting a precedent for Clyde steamers carrying passengers on recreational trips to the lower Clyde. Walter Scott was an early traveller when he went from Greenock to Glasgow in 1814, 'A journey which we performed at the rate of about eight miles an hour, and with a smooth-

ness of motion which probably resembles flying' (21).

By April 1825, 53 steamboats operated on the Clyde. Six years later *Lumsden's Steamboat Companion* lists 61, operating services down the Clyde from Glasgow to Dumbarton and Greenock, to various places in the Highlands and Islands such as Inveraray and as far as Iona and Staffa. Rothesay was already the destination of much of the Clyde traffic and her first steamboat pier had been built in 1815. The *Steamboat Companion* describes Rothesay:

'During summer, it is crowded with people from Glasgow and other places, who resort to it for the benefit of sea bathing: and during winter and spring, it has become the favourite resort of invalids, and particularly those who are threatened with consumption.'

Larger vessels, of more than 100 tons, took passengers to Liverpool, Dublin and Belfast.

David Napier was another great innovator, starting many services in the Firth. In 1828, in

20 The puffer *Auld Reekie* at Inverary in 1992.

order to get to his property at Glenshellish, he built a pier at Kilmun on the Holy Loch, 'which was then in a state of nature'. He constructed a steam carriage to take him overland to Loch Eck then a boat to cross the Loch. The service also continued to Inverary. The steam carriage was not a success, but the route was revived in the 1870s, when it was advertised as the 'famed Loch Eck route'.

By 1841, the steamboats had an ally and a rival for the traffic of the upper Clyde, when the Glasgow, Paisley and Greenock Railway (later part of the Caledonian Railway) opened its station at Greenock and linked it with steamers from Custom House Wharf nearby. The wealthy middle classes, looking for a quick route to their villas in the lower Firth, preferred this much faster service.

An even faster route to Rothesay opened in 1864, when the Greenock and Wemyss Bay

Railway Company (also absorbed into the Caledonian Railway) reached the latter port. In 1869 the Glasgow and South Western Railway completed its line to Princes Pier, Greenock, providing a shorter transit distance between train and ship, and a shorter sea journey, than the Caledonian Railway. On the north bank of the Clyde, the North British Railway attempted a link with steamships, but its terminus at Helensburgh was some distance from the pier and there was no space for development. In 1883 it opened a new double pier at Craigendoran, where the existing railway ran close to the shore. Finally, in 1889 the Caledonian leap-frogged the competition by building the longest tunnel in Scotland to reach Gourock, where steamers left from a spacious pier.

Often the railway companies formed their own steamship lines, as when the Caledonian Railway found no-one suitable to run its services from Gourock and set up the Caledonian Steam Packet Company. But such ventures were not always successful, and in many cases

21 A steamboat passing Dumbarton Castle among a crowd of sailing boats, from William Daniell's *Voyage Round Great Britain*, published from 1814 to 1825.

shipping companies such as G & J Burns and Williamson-Buchanan Ltd co-operated with the railways.

An 'all the way' service from the Broomielaw in Glasgow survived as a day excursion for the working classes of the city, attracting many complaints. Drunken Glaswegians were not welcome in the genteel resorts. According to Captain Andrew McQueen, 'Travellers by these boats were almost entirely "drouths", out to secure the alcoholic refreshment denied them ashore. The boats were simply floating "pubs"'. At the same time, philanthropists organized excursions for poor children of the city. Concerts, such as a performance of Handel's *Messiah*, took place on board special trips.

The Confederates in the American Civil War (1861–5) hired many Clyde steamers as blockade runners, leaving a gap which was filled by a new generation. Older steamers had

22 The *Mars* of 1845, a Clyde steamer of the earlier period, with no cabins above deck level. She is passing Toward Lighthouse south of Dunoon.

followed sailing ships in having little super-structure, but the new steamers were constructed differently. The second *Iona* of 1863 had a large deck saloon which greatly increased passenger comfort and became a feature of the ships. Bows were fine and canoe-like, though they had problems in rough water. In 1892 the *Glen Sannox* was built with a much higher bow and this too became standard.

As well as competition between the railway companies, there was intense rivalry between the individual ships. As *The Glasgow Herald* reported in 1888:

'Both steamers left Rothesay Pier at the same time, the *Lord of the Isles* having, if anything, the advantage. As Ardbeg Point was reached, the *Columba*, on the outside berth,

23 The late nineteenth-century type of steamer, the *Columba* of 1878 off Dunoon about 1900. Her decks and cabins are crowded with passengers.

forged ahead and crept up on the stern of the *Lord of the Isles*, the clouds of smoke emitted from the funnels gradually changed to flame. When fairly into the Kyles she passed the *Lord of the Isles*, winning, so to speak, a stern race by two boat lengths. *Columba*'s passengers cheered vociferously.'

Competition was slightly reduced by the end of the century, as companies began to see the advantages of co-operation. In 1923 the government forced the railway companies to merge into four large groups, with the London, Midland and Scottish taking over the services from the ports south of the river, and the London and North Eastern Railway operating from Craigendoran.

The Clyde steamer operators had an ambivalent attitude to new technology. The *King Edward*, the first commercial turbine ship, was used on the Ardrossan to Campbeltown route from 1901. On the other hand, the last paddler, the *Waverley*, was launched in 1946. Diesels were introduced in 1953 with a new class of ship, the *Maids of Ashton, Argyll, Skelmorlie* and *Cumbrae*, but the ships were not popular – there was too much vibration and the spectacle of the steam engines was eliminated.

MacBrayne's in the islands

Tourist trips to the Western Isles began very early in the history of the steamboat and indeed Henry Bell's *Comet* was lost in the Dorus Mor near Crinan in 1820. In 1839 Robert Napier began a 'swift steamer' service, with one boat travelling from Glasgow to Ardrishaig, a fast horse-drawn boat through the Crinan Canal and another fast steamer to

Oban, where the traveller could find vessels going to the tourist spots of Staffa, Iona and Glencoe. Until the middle of the century J & G Burns, also dominant on the Glasgow to Belfast route, were the principal operators, but in 1851 they sold their fleet to David Hutcheson, who formed a new company. One of his employees, David MacBrayne, became a partner and then took over the firm in 1879, bringing one of the most famous and lasting names to the Scottish islands.

'All the way' excursions by single ship from Glasgow and 'swift steamer' services connecting with Oban and Fort William were still the mainstay of the business, but in 1888 MacBrayne's took on mail contracts for the islands, beginning mail and passenger services to Mull and the outer isles from Oban, which was now on the railway system. In the 1890s the railways reached Fort William, Kyle of Lochalsh and Mallaig and MacBrayne's started steam ferries to Skye.

Scots in the world

Many thousands of Scots left the country over the centuries, usually by sea. In the eighteenth century emigrants, often from the Highlands, generally travelled in groups in chartered ships, sometimes from tiny ports. Even before Culloden, the tenants of the Campbell lands in Argyll were encouraged to emigrate. In 1738–40 Captain Lachlan Campbell of Islay persuaded 840 people to go to New York colony. The first ship, in 1738, carried 470 passengers. In 1773–6, 62 passengers left from Lochindaal in Islay, 136 from Lochbroom and 547 from the tiny island of Gigha.

On visiting an emigrant ship in Portree in 1773, Boswell found that the passengers lived in 'a long ward' with square, four-person beds on each side. The accommodation was 'very good'. But the voyage could be horrific. The following year Miss Janet Schaw sailed from Burntisland in the *Jamaica Packet*. As cabin passengers, she and her family were uncomfortable enough:

'Our bed-chamber, which is dignified with the title of State-room, is about five feet (1.5 m) wide and six (1.8 m) long; on one side is a bed fitted up for Miss Rutherford and on the opposite side one for me. Poor Fanny's is so very narrow, that she is forced to be tied in to prevent her falling over.'

But she found that another group of passengers, travelling secretly in the hold with the connivance of the captain, had infinitely worse conditions:

'I ought not to complain, when I see the poor Emigrants, to which our living is luxury. It is hardly possible to believe that human nature could be so depraved, as to treat fellow creatures in such a manner for a little sordid gain. They have only for a grown person per week, one pound neck beef, or spoilt pork, two pounds oatmeal, with a small quantity of bisket.'

Not all eighteenth-century emigrants were willing, as readers of Stevenson's *Kidnapped* will be aware. Though Scots were not involved in the Slave Trade from West Africa, they operated their own on a much smaller scale. Peter Williamson was eight years old when he was kidnapped in Aberdeen, taken to America and sold for £16. He eventually gained his freedom,

24 The Caledonian MacBrayne ferry in rough weather at Fionnphort, Sound of Iona, in January 1993.

made good and returned to Scotland, but there is no way of knowing how many suffered a worse fate.

The largest group of enforced emigrants were the prisoners of the '45 Rebellion. Nine hundred and thirty-six persons, about a quarter of the total captured, were transported to the colonies, mostly as 'indentured' servants. They sailed from English ports, in conditions which caused a third to die on some ships. Common criminals were also transported to America, though in much smaller numbers: voyages were so irregular that some prisoners languished for years in Scottish tollbooths. After American independence, transportation to Australia began in 1788. The most famous transportees were Thomas Muir and the Scottish Martyrs, convicted of sedition in 1793 and sentenced to 14 years. Muir escaped three years later with American assistance.

In the second half of the nineteenth century, emigrants were carried by regular shipping lines, in much improved conditions, though the 'steerage' passengers saw nothing of the luxury of first-class accommodation. In August 1879 Robert Louis Stevenson travelled to America. Arriving at Greenock by boat from the

Broomielaw he saw the Anchor Line's *Devonia* as 'a wall of bulwark, an aspiring forest of spars, larger than a church, and soon to be as populous as many an incorporated town in the land to which she was to bear us' (25). Though a second-class passenger, he befriended the emigrants in the steerage, who lived during a ten-day voyage in an area:

'...shaped like an isosceles triangle, the sides opposite the equal angles bulging outward with the contour of the ship. It is lined with eight pens of sixteen bunks apiece, four bunks below and four above on either side.' (26)

Enjoying an impromptu dance led by a fiddler, Stevenson saw the full force of Victorian class distinctions:

'Through this merry and good-hearted scene there came three cabin passengers, a gentleman and two young ladies, picking their way with little gracious titters of indulgence, and a Lady Bountiful air about nothing, which galled me to the quick.'

Sailing ships continued, especially on the longer routes. In 1884 the *Otago* of the Shire Line took four months to carry 37 crew and 361 passengers from the Clyde to Brisbane and the passengers complained of bad food, poor hygiene and the negligence of the surgeon (27).

25 The *Ethiopia*, sister ship to the *Devonia* in which Robert Louis Stevenson sailed to America in 1879.

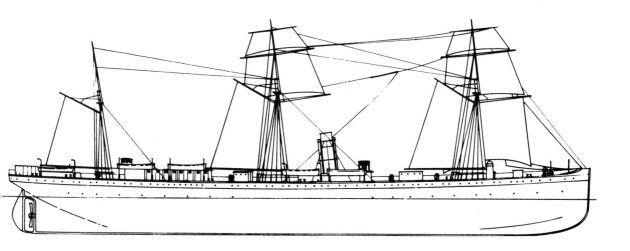

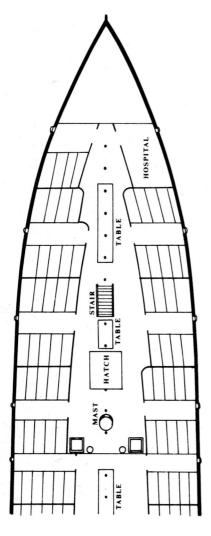

26 The steerage compartment of the *Ethiopia*. It is slightly different from Stevenson's description of the steerage, though he did not exaggerate. There were no more than seven tiers of bunks, though some were five deep instead of four.

Scottish shipping lines

In the days of sail, a ship was usually divided into 64 shares which were purchased by various individuals. One person might have an interest in several ships, but it was rare for anyone, except her master, to own a single ship; the risk of loss was too great. With the coming of steam and the joint-stock company in the 1830s and 1840s, shareholders invested in shipping companies rather than a ship. Even

so, the system of 64ths survived. Sir William Burrell, the famous art collector, for example, continued to have shares in a variety of ships, operating as managing owner on behalf of the other shareholders.

Steamships needed a high level of investment. Government mail contracts and rate-fixing conferences by shipowners helped to establish regular services throughout the world, demanding several ships on each to keep up a timetable. The larger shipowners tended to run 'liner' services, carrying passengers or cargo to schedule. Other ships became 'tramps', with no fixed routes, mainly carrying bulk cargoes such as coal.

Shipping companies worked hard to establish group identities. Each had its own 'house flag' and often a distinctive hull colouring and painted funnel. Many named their ships to a common theme, such as the Clan and Ben Lines. The setting up of a company generally demanded a shrewd, enterprising and strong-willed founder or set of partners. Scotland was to produce a supply of such men in the nineteenth century.

Some entrepreneurs started in Scotland but soon found the market too small for them. Samuel Cunard went into partnership with three Scots, including Robert Napier the Clyde shipbuilder, in 1839, but they operated transatlantic mail liners from Liverpool. Arthur Anderson, co-founder of Peninsular and Orient (P&O), was an Orcadian, but his fleet was based in London. Elder, Dempster, Glen and Shire lines also had Scottish connections, but were essentially English.

Among the companies which remained close to their Scottish base was Patrick Henderson. The founder built his first ship, the *Peter Senn*, in 1834, but died six years later; the last of the family died in 1868. However, the line was known ever after as 'Paddy Henderson'. Initially, it traded between Glasgow and the Mediterranean, then to India, Australia, New Zealand and Burma.

The Ben Line originated in 1839, when two brothers, Alexander and William Thomson,

27 Emigrants on board the sailing ship *Otago* on the way from the Clyde to Queensland in 1884. Their numbered bunks are behind.

built a small sailing ship to trade with Italy. They built their first steamship, the *Glenledi*, in 1871, but continued in sail until 1898. The 'Ben' names were established in the 1890s. Until 1919 they used 'one ship accounting': at the end of each voyage the profits were distributed to shareholders. Based in Leith, the Ben Line traded mainly in timber from Canada and the Baltic, with services to the Far East and South America.

The Anchor Line, founded by the Handyside Brothers and Thomas Henderson in 1852, was the most Scottish of all the international shipping lines. From an office in Union Street, Glasgow, it ran cargo services from Glasgow to New York and India, as well as passenger services to the Mediterranean and Canada (28). In 1907 it moved to new premises in St Vincent Place, with an imposing façade and rooms reflecting the luxury of an ocean liner. Their largest ship before World War I, the *Transylvania*, was of more than 14,000 tons, 549 ft (167 m) long and carried 305 first-class passengers, 216 second-class and 1858, mainly emigrants, in third class. She operated mostly in the Cunard livery, as part of a joint service.

The Allan brothers, sons of a ship's carpenter turned shipowner from Saltcoats, introduced their first steamer between Glasgow and

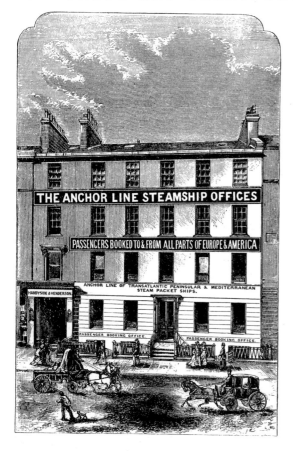

28 The Anchor Line offices at 51 Union Street, Glasgow, c.1870.

1857 the Indian Mutiny demonstrated the possibilities of government trooping contracts and after that all their ships were designed to be converted to carry soldiers; they took men to most of the small wars of Queen Victoria's reign. In 1863 the company was one of the first to introduce uniforms for its officers and crews. It was quick to see the opportunity for steam when the Suez Canal opened in 1869.

Some businessmen came from outside Scotland. Charles Cayzer, for example, was a Londoner who travelled the world as an employee of various shipping companies. Seeing the need for a direct service between industrial Clydeside and India, he went to Glasgow in 1877 and ordered the first two ships for the Clan Line in the following year. The *Clan MacAlpine* made her first voyage to India in October. The line specialized in cargo ships, but with high-quality accommodation for 12 passengers.

Christian Salvesen came to Scotland from Norway in 1843 at the age of 16 and in 1872 he became head of a company, owning ships as well as chartering them in the Norway-Scotland trade.

Shipping companies in faraway British colonies could be managed from Glasgow. James Galbraith never visited the east but he was the prime mover in the Irrawaddy Flotilla Company, which operated a fleet of up to 100 vessels, mostly shallow-draught paddle steamers, on the great river of Burma. Much less happily, William Denny III, one of the most inventive Scottish shipbuilders, was driven to suicide by difficulties in setting up La Platense Company in Argentina.

By 1912, there were six Glasgow shipping lines among the world's top 50, though none could be called a giant. The largest, Clan Line, operated 56 ships of 238,000 tons, compared with Hamburg-American at 908,000 tons and White Star of Liverpool with 495,000 tons. Even so, Scotland was punching above her weight in the world shipping market and even in United Kingdom terms. In 1910 she had 13.3 per cent of tonnage arriving at British

Montreal in 1854. By 1880 they had 39 ships, including iron sailing vessels. In 1912 they operated 25 ships of 186,000 tons.

The brothers William and John Donaldson, aged 26 and 23, bought their first sailing ship in 1858 and began trade between Glasgow and South America. In 1870, when they owned or chartered 16 vessels, they decided to go into steam and began a service to Canada in 1874. In 1913 they purchased the South American services of the Allan Line and from 1916, operated jointly with them.

The British India Steam Navigation Company began in Glasgow in 1856, with the purchase of the steamers *Baltic* and *Cape of Good Hope* by Robert Mackinnon and William Mackenzie, both from Campbeltown, who had worked as shipping agents in India. In

29 The *Bardic Ferry* being prepared for launch at Dumbarton

ports, and just over 10 per cent of exports by value.

Scottish shipowners supported high-profile artistic and cultural projects: Sir William Burrell gave his famous art collection to the City of Glasgow and Sir James Caird financed the new National Maritime Museum in Greenwich, London. Both these men, however, symbolized the decline of Scottish shipping: they were rich because they had got out at the right moment, Burrell in 1901 and Caird in 1917.

The great days of the Scottish shipping lines were over by 1914. British India moved its head office to London in 1882. Salvesen of Leith went into whaling and became the largest whaling group in the world by 1911. The increasing size of the great Atlantic liners, especially after 1900, led to concentration of trade in Liverpool and later Southampton. Scottish shipping declined faster after 1918

because its industrial base was weaker and because financial and commercial control centred more on London. Anchor Line went into liquidation in 1935, though the name survived under different management. Clan Line remained a family business until 1956, when it merged with Union Castle. The Allan Line was wound up in 1967.

Modern ferries

When Denny of Dumbarton launched the *Bardic Ferry* in 1957, her builders could not have been aware of the effect such ships would soon have on the Highlands and Islands (29). She was the first purpose-built roll-on roll-off (ro-ro) ferry, though converted wartime landing ships had been used. Built for service between the North of England and Ireland, she formed a contrast with three ships already operating in the Firth of Clyde – the car ferries *Arran*, *Bute* and *Cowal*. Built a few years earlier, each had its own vehicle lift. This made it unnecessary to redesign every pier where the ships might operate, but it was far too slow and in the holiday season it was necessary to book a car's passage weeks in advance. The system used in the *Bardic Ferry*, was far superior and in 1970 the Clyde got its own ro-ro in the shape of the *Caledonia*, converted from a three-year-old Norwegian ship for the Arran route. The *Arran* was converted in 1972. By 1993 CalMac, formed by a merger between the Caledonian Steam Packet Company and MacBrayne's in 1973, was operating 28 car ferries in the Clyde and to the islands. They ranged in size from the *Caledonian Isles* which could carry 110 cars, to the *Eigg* which could take five. They carried 1.3 million cars a year. Their only rival was Western Ferries, which began with a short-lived service to Islay in 1968, but now operates a utilitarian service to Dunoon.

Since motorists prefer to spend their time in their own cars rather than a ferry, the short sea crossings tend to dominate: the Western Ferries service across the Clyde to Dunoon, for example, is advertised as 'The Short Crossing'. Sometimes this can lead to disaster: when Orkney District Council decided to set up a service between Gills Bay in Caithness and Burwick on South Ronaldsay, with both ends affected by the enormous currents of the Pentland Firth, it ignored the advice of local pilots to its cost. £1.8m was budgeted to build the terminals, but this rose to £3.2m. It was then found that another £6m was needed, so the service never started. The ferry to Stromness is much more successful, as is the much longer route from Aberdeen to Stromness, an exception to the general rule about the shortest crossing being the most popular in the days of the motor car.

3
Ports and Harbours

Natural harbours

A harbour is simply an area where ships can find shelter from wind and weather. There are many such places round the coast of Scotland, in sea lochs, among groups of islands, or in river mouths. In its simplest form it is a natural anchorage, or 'road', where the water is deep enough for the ship to float but shallow enough for an anchor to be effective, with a bottom in which the anchor will take hold; with reasonably easy entry and exit and with protecting land all around. According to Graeme Spence surveying Scapa Flow in 1812, 'The good properties of a roadstead ought to be six ... namely capacity, shelter, depth of water, good ground, easy access and little tide'.

As well as providing refuge from storms, an anchorage would be used by sailing ships awaiting a favourable wind, and merchant ships could unload by transferring their cargo to small barges. The value of an anchorage is related to the size of the ships using it. Scapa Flow contains 120 square miles of water and was invaluable for the great battleships of the Grand Fleet in 1914, but yachtsmen much prefer tiny havens such as Caladh Harbour in the Kyles of Bute or Canna Harbour in the Hebrides.

A beach is another simple harbour. Early Scottish craft, such as curraghs, Viking ships and West Highland galleys, could be drawn up out of the water, while larger or heavier vessels could be grounded at high tide and then left high and dry at low water. The Clyde puffer had a flat bottom so that it could operate on the beaches of Islay as well as in the more sophisticated facilities of Glasgow. A small natural indentation among the rocks can also be used as a harbour, as at Staxigoe in Caithness; such harbours tend to be small, capable of some improvement but not much expansion.

A port is more than a harbour, for in addition to its provision of shelter, it has facilities to conduct trade. Most anchorages are too open for this, so early ports, such as Ayr, Berwick, Aberdeen and Leith, were generally situated at the mouths of small rivers. As bigger ships were built over the years and rivers tended to get shallower because of the deposit of human waste in them, old ports such as Perth and Stirling declined.

As important as anything else in the development of a port is its hinterland. In 1540, Alexander Lindsay believed that Cromarty Firth was 'above all hauens in the yle of Britane for saifftie of shippis both great and small', but it was never of national importance until recent times. Conversely, Leith and Glasgow are unpromising sites from a maritime point of view, but both were developed by vast investment to serve the towns and regions close to them.

There was often conflict between the ports near the mouth of the river and those further upstream at the first bridge. For centuries Dumbarton tried to exercise its medieval right to levy tolls on ships passing up to Glasgow and to hinder the deepening of the Clyde – to little avail for the town was completely eclipsed by what became the 'Second City' of the British Empire. Perth, on the other hand, was outgrown by Dundee, despite centuries of legal dispute. In 1600, for example, Perth was granted the right 'that na ship coming within the river should break bulk [ie open its hold] until it came to the [Perth] Bridge, unless it be loadened with goods belonging to the inhabitants of Dundee'. Within two years Dundee had overturned this restriction on its trade and Perth became a market town rather than a seaport, though as late as 1870 its fathers insisted that the height under the proposed Tay Bridge be set at 100 ft (30.5 m) so that the tallest ships could go up river.

Improvements of ports

The simplest way to improve a river port was to build up its banks behind a wall, creating an area of deeper water to which ships could come alongside and perhaps remain afloat as the tide fell, as well as an area of land in which goods could be stored and sorted. A map of Aberdeen in 1661 shows the north bank of the Dee with 'drye-grounde sometyme overflowed

30 Greenock and Port Glasgow showing the sandbanks and anchorages, from John Watt's survey of 1734.

by the Tyde befor the Peer was builded'. The 'Peer' was not the type later known in Scotland, jutting out at right angles to the bank, but a wall along the side of the river.

A breakwater built out into the sea could greatly improve the shelter offered by a port in an exposed position. One was built at Crail in Fife around 1500, possibly replacing an older one. It can still be seen and is identifiable from its rough masonry, though it is now surmounted by a nineteenth-century wall and ends with a structure of 1862, with another breakwater protecting the entrance. It was also possible to improve a harbour by cutting into the land, as at Dunbar in the early eighteenth century, where 8 ft (2.4 m) was cut into solid rock on the foreshore and a sandstone pier built to protect the entrance. This made it a safe harbour, though small and difficult to enter.

By 1700 Leith was the most important Scottish port, serving Edinburgh and as an entrepôt for the trade of Fife and Lothian with the Netherlands. It was based on the mouth of the Water of Leith, improved by building up the banks and constructing jetties on each side of the entrance, but the sand still dried out at low water more than half a mile from the entrance.

Meanwhile on the other side of Scotland,

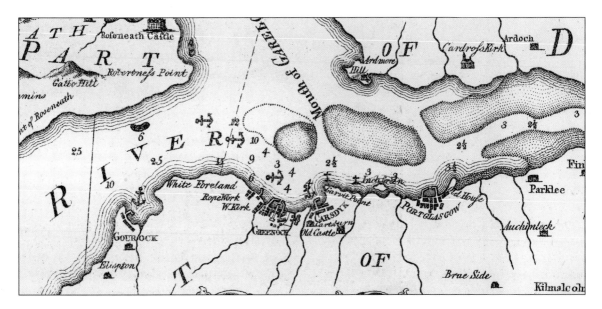

the merchants of Glasgow needed an outlet to the sea. Since the sixteenth century they had used the Ayrshire port of Irvine, but the River Irvine there was shallow and narrow. In 1667 Dumbarton rebuffed them on the grounds that the influx of seafarers would raise the price of provisions, but in the following year, despite opposition from nearby Greenock, Glasgow purchased land near Newark Castle with a view to setting up her own port. It was 1693, however, before detailed plans were drawn up and the new harbour of Port Glasgow, formed by two breakwaters with a central pier, was begun. It later included Scotland's first dry dock for the repair of ships and a new town was built behind it. Glasgow merchants were obliged to load and unload their ships at Port Glasgow, rather than at any other port on the Clyde (30).

Later, Port Glasgow began to belie its name. Greenock was in a more favourable position in relation to the Tail of the Bank anchorage and had more room for expansion. Sir John Shaw succeeded in liberating the town from feudal restrictions and a new harbour was built by his son from 1707 to 1710. As the channel up to Glasgow was improved throughout the eighteenth and nineteenth centuries, Port Glasgow's original purpose was removed and it developed as a centre of shipbuilding rather than trade.

The great engineers

In the second half of the eighteenth century and the first part of the nineteenth, Scottish harbours were improved by a number of notable engineers. Often several of them worked in succession on the same harbours: Smeaton, Telford and Rennie at Aberdeen, Rennie and Telford on deepening the Clyde.

John Smeaton (1724–92), an Englishman of Scottish descent, did most of his work south of the border, notably the third Eddystone Lighthouse off Plymouth. In Scotland he supervised the construction of the Forth and Clyde Canal and developed the harbours at Peterhead and Cromarty. In 1769–70 he made the first improvements to the navigation of Aberdeen.

He reported:

'The principal complaint attending to this Harbour, is the difficulty of entry, occasioned by a Bar a little without the Harbour mouth; and a shifting bed of sand, gravel and shingle, on the north side of the entry; by which action of the seas, when the wind is in the north-easterly quarter, drives into the main channel, choking it up in different degrees...'

He recommended a training wall be built from the north bank of the River Dee into the North Sea to direct the flow of the river into a particular channel.

Thomas Telford (1757–1834) was a Scot from Eskdale. He carried out a vast amount of work in England, where he was a founder of the Institute of Civil Engineers. In Scotland, he was the main engineer for the Caledonian Canal, built between 1804 and 1822. His largest body of work in Scotland began in 1790, when he was appointed Surveyor of the Buildings to the British Fisheries Society. In this role he built new towns and harbours at Ullapool and at Pultneytown near Wick. There were few harbours in the north of Scotland which did not see Telford's improving hand over a period of more than 40 years.

John Rennie (1761–1821) was also a Scot, from East Lothian, who worked extensively in Scotland and England. In his native land he was perhaps best known for bridge-building, though his harbour improvements were executed at Alloa, St Andrews, Berwick, Charlestown and Greenock.

Glasgow and the Clyde

The greatest achievement of the age was the deepening of the River Clyde. In 1755 it had only 18 in (0.5 m) of water in places at low tide and even small barges had great difficulty in reaching Glasgow (31). The Glasgow merchants, disturbed by the failure of Port Glasgow and the rivalry of Greenock, employed John Smeaton, who proposed a large dam and lock at Marlinford, near Scotstoun, which would give 4 ft 6 in (1.3 m) of water at all times in Glasgow Harbour. This was

31 The unimproved Clyde above Dumbarton, drawn by John Slezer in the late seventeenth century.

opposed by many, including those who forded the river rather than paying dues for ferries or bridges, and never implemented: with hindsight, it would have restricted the growth of the harbour, for it was designed for ships of up to only 100 tons.

In 1768 an English engineer named John Golborne was asked to report. He suggested a radical scheme, in which the river would have its flow increased by restricting the width of the main channel, scouring out the bottom and increasing the depth. A further survey by James Watt confirmed the practicality of this and an Act of Parliament was passed in 1770 allowing Glasgow to build stone dykes out from each bank, narrowing the channel to about 300 ft (approx 90 m) in many places. Between Dumbarton and Bowling the Lang Dyke was built to close off one of two channels and train the water along the north side (colour plate 2).

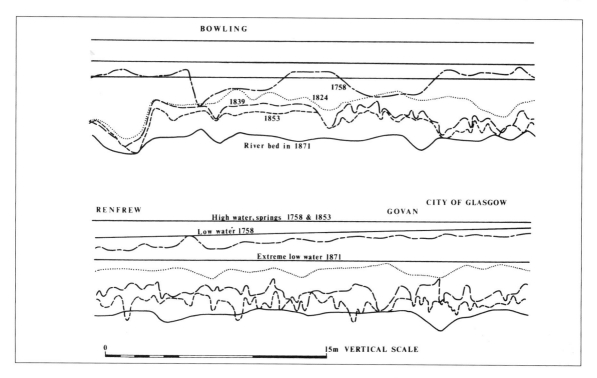

BOWLING

1758

1839   1824

1853

River bed in 1871

RENFREW   GOVAN   CITY OF GLASGOW

High water, springs 1758 & 1853

Low water 1758

Extreme low water 1871

0   15m VERTICAL SCALE

32 The depths in the River Clyde between Dumbuck and Glasgow Bridge in 1758, 1824, 1853 and 1871.

As a result, 7 ft (2.1 m) of water could be guaranteed up to Glasgow on an ordinary high tide.

This began a long process of improvement. In 1799 John Rennie reported that Golborne's dykes, built without any scientific means of predicting their effect, needed some modifications. Thomas Telford recommended some alterations to the Lang Dyke in 1806 and the following year Rennie suggested that the spaces between the projecting dykes allowed silt to settle. On his recommendation, the ends of the dykes were joined together over the next 30 years, with dykes parallel to the flow of the river, and land behind them was reclaimed. In 1836 it was reported that there was a minimum of 7 or 8 ft (2.1 or 2.4 m) at low water at the Broomielaw in the heart of Glasgow.

By this time it was realized that constricting the river had gone too far. In 1824 Joseph Whidbey claimed that the lack of tidal flow was actually hindering the deepening of the river, while sailors were finding the channel too narrow for the traffic it was carrying. In 1836 the Clyde Trustees began a programme of widening and straightening,

digging out and dredging the banks behind the parallel dykes. By the 1870s, the Clyde offered a minimum depth of 21 ft (6.4 m) up to Glasgow, with a channel 300 ft (90 m) wide. Whereas Smeaton had hoped for a river navigable by ships of 100 tons, the Clyde could now take the largest ships of the day, up to 4000 tons (32).

There was immense pride in the development of the river. A conference in Glasgow in 1901 was told, 'There is no Scotchman who is not stirred to his inmost core at the great achievements which have been made on the Clyde'. As the saying has it, 'The Clyde made Glasgow and Glasgow made the Clyde'.

The steam dredger

Before steam power, it was very difficult to deepen a river by dredging. The 'spoon and bag' type used a large amount of labour to remove a small amount of spoil from the bottom. On the Clyde, Golborne used machines based on the principle of the plough. 'They are large hollow cases. ... They are drawn across the river by means of capstans, placed on long wooden frames or planks.' The Dutch developed a mechanical dredger in the seventeenth century, using buckets which were rotated round a ladder by human or horse power. In 1798, before steam power was applied to the propulsion of ships, a 4 horsepower engine was fitted to a dredger at Sunderland.

Partly because Golborne's dykes seemed effective, the Clyde was quite slow to adopt the steam dredger. One was used at Dundee in 1810 and another in the construction of the Caledonian Canal a few years later, but it was 1824 before the Clyde Trustees ordered their first. The unnamed vessel was 59 ft (18 m) long and could dredge to 10 ft 6 in (3.2 m). Her 12 horsepower engine powered the dredging equipment, but she had to be moved by means of anchors and moorings laid out ahead. By 1865, *dredger no 8* had 75 horsepower and

could dredge to 28 ft (8.5 m). Spoil was put into a hopper barge which was towed out to the mouth of Loch Long where its bottom was opened and the spoil emptied into the water.

Dredger no 9 of 1871 was the first to be built by the shipyard of William Simons at Renfrew, introducing the company to a trade which was to become its speciality (33). Simons had already made their first contribution to the techniques of dredging in 1861, by building the world's first self-propelled hopper barges. Over the years the firm would build many dredgers for the world market, in rivalry with Lobnitz, their neighbours on the Renfrew shore.

As ships became larger, dredging was increasingly necessary to keep the Clyde viable as a port and a shipbuilding river. There was alarm in 1854 when hard rock, rather than soft clay, was exposed near Elderslie, and new techniques of underwater blasting were needed. Special measures had to be taken in 1914 when the 49,000 ton *Aquitania*, the Clyde's biggest ship so far, was taken down river from Clydebank. When the Queen Mary made the same journey in 1936, the Trustees had been

33 *No 9 Dredger* built by Simons of Renfrew for the River Clyde in 1871.

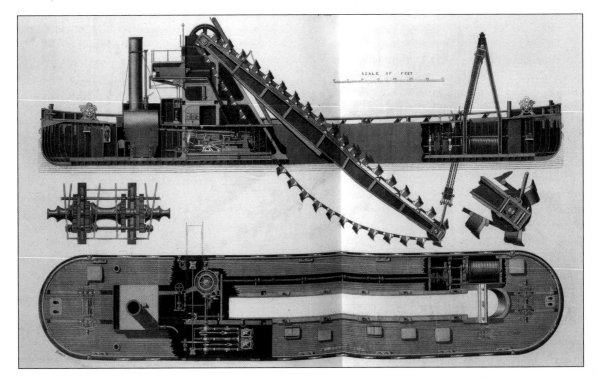

carrying out extra dredging for several years. A high spring tide was chosen, the ship was lightened to a draught of 35 ft (10.7 m), but even so she grounded off Dalmuir. There was great tension for several minutes until tugs freed her before a falling tide could make the situation much worse.

Dredgers worked on the approach channels at most Scottish ports. James Rendel reported on work at Leith in 1853:

'The new dredging vessel is an excellent one and now working most satisfactorily. ... whereas the cost of dredging used to be upwards of 8d per cubic yard, the cost has been reduced to about 5d per yard. ... I find that about 1,000 ft [305 m] of the Harbour Channel have been nearly completed, and that the remainder of it has progressed so far that it is within three feet [0.9 m] of its intended depth.'

Tugs

Since the steamship grew up on the River Clyde, it is no surprise that the steam tug was in very early use. The *Charlotte Dundas* might claim to be the first tug, in that she hauled barges on the Forth and Clyde Canal in 1802, although the idea was not taken up on the grounds that her wash would damage the banks. The *Industry* of 1814, built at Fairlie in Ayrshire, was designed as a passenger boat, then used as a luggage carrier between Glasgow and the Firth, but soon after 1815 she began to tow barges. The very word 'tug' comes from the name of a vessel built by Denny of Dumbarton in 1817: the *Tug* was intended to tow ships on the Forth between Leith and Grangemouth. In the following year the Clyde Shipping Company, 'being sensible of the uncertain, inconvenient mode of carrying goods up the Clyde to Glasgow, resolved to have built and fitted up in an elegant fashion, a handsome and stout steam vessel called the *Samson* with accommodation for passengers and for towing lighters laden with goods' (34).

The earliest tugs were built of wood, in similar form to other ships of the day, and propelled by paddles. The first iron paddle tug in

34 The engine of the *Clyde* paddle steamer, built in 1851 by A & J Inglis as a tug for the Clyde Navigation Trust.

Scotland was the *Wizard*, used at Glasgow from 1848. Leith introduced her first in 1853 and Dundee in 1865. Because tugs tended to operate in shallow and sheltered waters, paddle wheels on tugs survived longer than they did on seagoing vessels. The first screw tugs on the Clyde were the *Clyde*, *Forth*, *Tay* and *Tweed* of 1874–7, with a propeller at each end to increase manoeuvrability. More conventional screw tugs, intended to tow sailing ships out into the open sea as far as the south of Ireland, were introduced by the Clyde Shipping Company in 1880, but it was 1901 before the first screw tug started work on the Forth.

The steam tug had a profound effect on ship and harbour design. It soon graduated from towing barges to full-size sailing ships, so that the designers of the latter could now concentrate on deep-sea performance, while upriver ports such as Glasgow could develop yet further. As ocean-going steamships became more common in the last quarter of the nineteenth century, the role of the steam tug changed yet again. Though most ships could now make their own way into port, tugs were needed to manoeuvre them in tight spaces.

New harbours

Civil engineering techniques improved throughout the nineteenth century, greatly aided by the use of steam power for excavating and removing

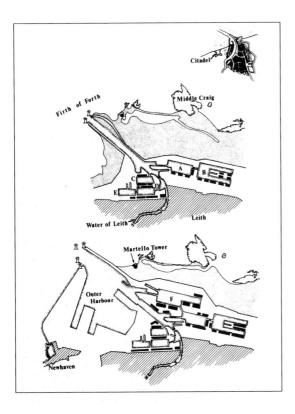

35 Leith Harbour in 1690, 1885 and 1948.

The idea of a 'harbour of refuge' was popular throughout the nineteenth century. It would have little trade of its own but would shelter all kinds of craft, from fishing boats to naval battleships, from storms. In 1886 Peterhead, strategically sited in the most easterly part of Scotland, was chosen for development with national funding. A great breakwater, 3000 ft (914 m) long was built, largely with convict labour, but the project was not completed until 1958, by which time weather forecasting made the concept obsolete.

The building of docks

In England, during the eighteenth century, enclosed docks gained favour in great ports such as Liverpool and London, for they created spaces inshore from the banks of rivers, where many more ships could be loaded and unloaded. Lock gates could be fitted to keep the ships away from the effects of the tides and the new docks were enclosed by walls, so creating far more secure conditions than on the river itself. In Scotland they were first introduced at Leith (35). The Old East Dock (as it later became) was begun in 1801 to the designs of Charles Rennie. It opened in 1806 and the Old West Dock was in use eleven years later.

At Dundee, the old harbour, dating from the fifteenth century, consisted of two 'havens' divided by a central pier, with two detached wooden breakwaters, or 'bulwarks' outside. These had needed extensive repair in the 1580s and 1640s, but by the early nineteenth century the harbour was described as 'a crooked wall, affording shelter to only a few fishing boats or smuggling vessels'. In 1815 an Act of Parliament was passed to modernize the harbour and new wet docks were opened in 1825 and 1834. Between 1863 and 1875 the Victoria and Camperdown Docks were built, offering enclosed and non-tidal spaces for ships in the rapidly expanding jute trade.

Grangemouth developed as a canal port at

spoil, the use of the steam dredger, and the development of the diving suit for underwater work.

Greenock expanded mainly by the building of new harbours out from the shore. The East India Dock was an expansion of Sir John Shaw's original harbour, designed by John Rennie. It was opened in 1805 and is largely intact today. Alongside, Victoria Harbour was built from 1846 to 1850 and Albert Harbour from 1862 to 1870, both open to the rise and fall of the tide.

An artificial harbour could be created by building a pair of curved breakwaters out until they almost met across the entrance. Such a harbour needed some means to scour it, to prevent it being gradually silted up with sand or mud. Port Glasgow, the earliest such harbour in Scotland, was already silting up by 1751. Port Edgar, built near South Queensferry in the late nineteenth century, had a similar problem. The 1914 Admiralty Pilot Book stated, 'The harbour dries out to its entrance point at low water springs, and is seldom used'.

36 Dunoon Pier in the early twentieth century, with the *Kenilworth* and *Talisman*.

the end of the Forth and Clyde, though it was opened in 1777, 13 years before the canal. It utilized the mouth of the River Carron and it benefited from traffic avoiding very high dues at Leith. In 1810 it ceased to be a 'creek' of Bo'ness for Customs purposes and became a head port in its own right. Its first wet dock, mainly for coastal shipping, was opened in 1843 and another, for foreign shipping, in 1859. The Carron Dock of 1882 more than doubled the water area of the port and was followed by the even larger Grange Dock in 1906. Grangemouth had a steady rise and was among the busiest ports in Scotland by 1910, with more than 1000 foreign-going ship movements per year.

These were true 'docks' or more strictly 'wet docks', fitted with gates or locks to maintain the water at a constant level. In Glasgow a different solution was adopted. In the old river harbour at Broomielaw in 1840, ships were moored nine or ten deep and the harbour was 'jammed from side to side, so that vessels could neither get up nor down' (colour plate 4). Since the port was far upriver in a waterway which was virtually a canal by 1870, it was decided that no gates were needed. Ships could come and go therefore at any state of the tide and the problems of a large body of stagnant, polluted water would be avoided. In 1880 Queen's Dock, to the north of the river, was opened, to be followed by the Princes Dock to the south in 1897. The open docks surprised other port operators. In 1901, the Engineer-in-Chief to the Trustees had to admit that the largest ships sometimes touched ground in the dock. The Manager of the Manchester Ship Canal commented that such an event in his waterway would cause 'a very serious disturbance'

The only true wet dock on the Clyde was the James Watt Dock, built at Greenock in 1886, at the height of the fashion for such docks in the other ports of Britain, but it cost

37 The pier at Kilmun on the Holy Loch.

the enormous sum of £850,000. The Great Harbour was built alongside, with an area of 58 acres (23.5 hectares) compared with 14 1/2 acres (5.7 hectares) for the wet dock. It was open to the north and served as a tidal basin.

In Aberdeen the harbour was close to the town centre and to the mouth of the river, so there was little room for expansion. The main aim was to improve the existing facilities rather than open up new ones. Quays were built along the river banks and the Victoria Dock was opened in 1848, the first wet dock in the port.

The Clyde steamer piers

As with many other things, David Napier can be credited with the invention of the Clyde steamer pier. His construction at Kilmun, intended to give access to his home in the area, still survives. The piers of the Firth of Clyde are unique in Britain (37). They are much shorter than the piers of English seaside resorts, because the shores are steeper. Unlike their English counterparts, they never developed into pleasure piers, for the steamship remained the best means of transport in the Firth, even in the railway age. In themselves, most piers provide no kind of shelter to ships. This is satisfactory in the relatively sheltered waters of the Firth, and with vessels which could disembark their passengers in a few minutes.

In the major ports, at Glasgow, Greenock, Port Glasgow and Gourock, steamers generally came alongside piers parallel to the line of the river. At other places, where port facilities were much less developed, a pier, usually constructed from wooden piles, projected from the shore. At Craigendoran, the depot of the North British Railway, a double pier allowed four steamers to moor at once, and provided some shelter for overnight moorings. At Rothesay, for long the greatest of the Clyde resorts, a Pi-shaped pier was built, mainly in the 1830s, with a drawbridge allowing access to an inner harbour. At Largs, one of the oldest piers, built in stone in 1832, is L-shaped and substantially

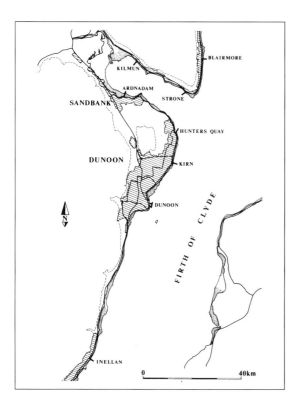

38 Piers in the Dunoon area.

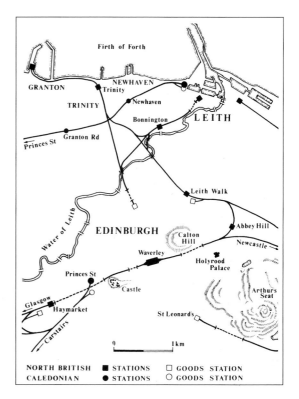

39 Railways in the Leith area, 1882.

intact, but at the smaller stops such as Roseneath, Kilcreggan, Blairmore and Auchenlochan, the T-shaped pier was the standard.

Transport links

Before the canal and railway, most ports were essentially local, serving a hinterland of a few miles by primitive road transport. This became less true with the rise of trade in expensive luxury goods. Thus Glasgow became the centre of an international market in tobacco, sent by road to the Firth of Forth at Bo'ness.

The point where a canal met the sea or river sometimes allowed the development of a new port, or the expansion of an old one. At the ends of the Caledonian Canal, opened in 1822, the established towns of Fort William and Inverness were somewhat boosted. On the Crinan Canal, opened in 1801, Ardrishaig developed into a large village, while Crinan at the other end remained a hamlet. On the

Forth and Clyde, Bowling gained quite a large harbour but never became a major port, while Grangemouth, alone among Scottish canal ports, developed well beyond that role and indeed continued to expand after the canal fell into disuse.

In the coalfields, the history of the railway is bound up with the ports. The first 'waggonways' were used for horse drawn waggons carrying coal to cities such as Glasgow, factories such as the Carron Iron Works, or ports for further shipment. The earliest was built in 1722, linking the pits at Tranent with Cockenzie on the Forth. Another, dating from 1767, carried coal from Dunfermline to Charlestown in Fife. The longest and by far the most sophisticated waggonway, opened in 1812, was from Kilmarnock to Troon.

When the steam railway came to Scotland, much of the network was still geared to moving coal from pithead to port. The railway and the steamship were equally strongly linked in the passenger trades of the River Clyde, as the main railway companies leap-frogged one another in creating rail links with piers.

In the non-specialized ports such as Leith and Glasgow, the position was much more complex. The rail routes were often far from ideal, because of the rivalry between different railway companies, because the system was built piecemeal and because much of the suitable land was already occupied. At Leith there were three separate lines leading out of the port from different stations: the Caledonian Railway towards the junction at Granton, the North British Line which followed the valley of the Water of Leith, and another North British station to the east of the harbour, leading towards Portobello. No line took the most obvious and direct route to Edinburgh, down Leith Walk.

In Glasgow the railway seemed unnecessary at first as the main quay at the Broomielaw was close to the city centre, while onward traffic largely used the Forth and Clyde Canal or was transferred to small craft for transport to the Highlands. In 1846 the Clyde Trustees expressed the hope that 'no railways of any kind be permit-

ted to be placed upon any part of the sheds or in the streets of the quays of the harbour of Glasgow'. It was only in 1886 that Queen's Dock was directly linked with the city centre.

Since the 1950s, links with road transport have been more important than rail. In contrast to rail, road transport tends to avoid the traffic congestion of city centres, which has contributed greatly to the decline of ports such as Glasgow and Leith and the rise of places such as Grangemouth which are close to motorways.

The coal ports

Coal was the original bulk cargo, needing large volumes of shipping to move it into an international market. The industry boomed in the late nineteenth century, with 515 Scottish pits producing 23 million tons in 1889. Of the four main Scottish coalfields, Ayrshire and Fife produced most for export and special ports were developed, with waggon and railway links to the pitheads and specialized equipment for

40 Methil Docks in the 1890s, with coal hoists in the background and coal waggons in the foreground.

loading coal onto ships.

Charlestown was the first of the Fife harbours to be improved for coal shipment, when the Earl of Elgin built an inner basin around 1770. An outer basin was added around 1840. In ancient times Burntisland formed a natural harbour, described in MacPherson's Annals of Commerce in 1805 as 'having great capacity for being a seat of commerce and manufactures. But it has little of either worth mentioning'. From 1876, two wet docks and a tidal basin were built. Methil Harbour was developed between 1887 and 1913 to become the busiest and most sophisticated of the Scottish coal ports (40). It had ten hydraulic hoists lifting coal trucks to tip their loads into a ship. In 1913 it handled more than 3 million tons.

In Ayrshire the older ports of Ayr and Irvine were used for shipment, largely to Ireland. Ayr was improved by dredging and by building a large dock in the late nineteenth century, and by fitting an electric coal conveyor. Irvine languished until 1873, when the bar at its mouth was reduced by building dykes.

Two new ports were created by aristocratic enterprise in the early nineteenth century: Ardrossan and Troon. Ardrossan was built by the Earl of Eglinton from 1806, as part of an abortive scheme to link up with Glasgow by canal, removing the need to deepen the Clyde. Ardrossan gained a sophisticated system of breakwaters and became a coal port during the nineteenth century, shipping more than a quarter of a million tons in 1855. It declined by the 1920s when the north Ayrshire coalfield was worked out. Troon, on the other hand, built by the Duke of Portland in 1808, was always designed as a coal port,. A pier was extended 500 ft (142 m) into the sea to improve the natural harbour and early in the twentieth century it was fitted with four coaling cranes.

Port equipment

Within a large port, individual docks specialized in different trades, and were fitted with equipment for handling different cargoes. Glasgow remained prejudiced against coal shipments within its immediate area, but the Trustees built a special site at Govan just outside the city. General Terminus Quay on the south bank at Govan was opened in 1849, served by a railway carrying coal from Lanarkshire. By 1907 the boundaries of the city had expanded and the new Rothesay Dock, 6 miles downriver from Glasgow, was opened specifically for coal shipment. Meadowside Granary was sited in Partick and had a capacity of 96,000 tons. Merklands Quay, opened in 1907, was for the transport of cattle and was fitted with storage pens, a slaughterhouse and cold store.

Port cranes varied in size, from the small hand-operated machines which can still be seen in ports such as Easdale off the island of Seil to the large steam cranes introduced during the nineteenth century (41). Hydraulic power was first used in Scotland in the 1840s, and was far more convenient than steam, while electric power was common by 1900. The most famous Scottish crane is at Finnieston, identical in style to the largest of the shipyard cranes and used to hoist heavy loads, especially locomotives, onto ships. Most port cranes, however, were of the luffing-jib type, mainly because the jib of a dockside crane had to be able to lift, to move among the masts of a fully rigged ship. In the early version the load itself had to be raised and lowered with the jib, wasting energy. This was solved by the 'level-luffing' jib, in which an arrangement of pulleys ensured that the load remained level.

Leith was heavily involved in the grain trade, importing nearly a quarter of a million tons in 1947–8. Edinburgh and Imperial Docks both had large grain warehouses and two pneumatic elevators were in operation, capable of handling 180 tons per hour.

Warehouses in Scottish ports tended to be small and simple compared with the grand edifices of London and Liverpool. Most were single or two-storey sheds, such as those at Yorkhill Quay in Glasgow. The offices of port authorities, on the other hand, reflected the splendour of Victorian enterprise. The Clyde

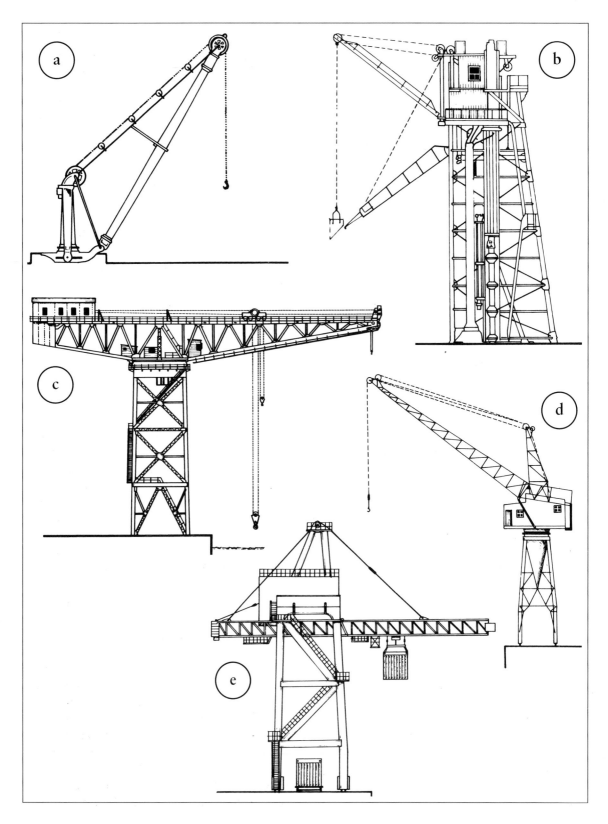

Port Authority offices in Robertson Street, Glasgow, are crowned by a dome and have the most sophisticated interiors in the city.

Customs

With the Union of 1707, Scotland was subjected to the high English duties on items such as wines and vinegar, tobacco, coffee and whale fins. Collectors were appointed, enjoined to 'take Notice that the Laws which are now the Standard of Trade and Duties have been constructed with very great Tenderness towards the Fair Trading Merchants, with very great Encouragements to Industry, and that the severities intended are for the prevention of Frauds, which can only be committed by Men of bad Principles'. Not many Scots agreed, and smuggling was almost a patriotic duty. When Andrew Wilson was hanged in Edinburgh in 1736 for robbing a Customs officer, it led to riots and the lynching of Captain Porteous of the Town Guard.

Amid such scenes of near anarchy, Customs Houses were built in the main ports, with a grandeur which symbolized the authority of the state. The Leith Customs House was built in 1812 to replace a much older one. At Greenock, the Customs House was built by William Burn in 1818 in a magnificent Doric style (colour plate 3). The Glasgow Customs House, built in 1840, is less successful, being described in the Glasgow volume of *The Buildings of Scotland* (Williamson *et al*) as having an 'unassuming Greek Revival façade of uncomfortable proportions'.

Initially, Scotland was divided into 17

41 Types of crane in Scottish ports:

a. A hydraulic crane installed for loading coal at General Terminus Quay, Glasgow, in 1850.

b. A coal hoist at Dundee.

c. The Fairfield Crane, installed in the shipyard in 1912.

d. An electric luffing jib quay crane, as used at Glasgow and many other ports.

e. A container crane at Grangemouth, the first to be installed in Britain.

Customs ports. A few had 'members', only slightly subordinate to the head port, such as Alloa to Bo'ness. All had 'creeks' where there was no permanent Customs presence. Montrose had ten creeks, including Arbroath, Auchmithie and Lunan Water, while Irvine had Largs, Portencross and Saltcoats.

Working in the ports

Work in the docks was essentially intermittent and seasonal, especially in the days of sailing ships when a large number might arrive together on a favourable wind and tide. Labour was taken on a casual basis, and conditions did not improve in the early twentieth century at a time when workers in other fields began to get more secure employment. Until containerization in the 1960s and 1970s most ships had 'break-bulk' cargoes which had to be unloaded largely by hand, creating a demand for a large semi-skilled labour force. Trade unions struggled hard to control the supply of labour, to prevent their own members being undercut in hard times.

Glasgow was the largest Scottish port at the beginning of the twentieth century, but never had more than 4000 dockers, compared with 28,000 on the Thames and 27,000 on the Mersey. For most of their history the Scottish unions marched to a slightly different tune from the English dockers. While the Leith men were affiliated to the National Union of Dock Labourers, the Scottish Union of Dock Labourers was the dominant force in Glasgow. The union had a particularly strong control of the labour force, so it felt no need for registration schemes as proposed in other ports: an anti-Registration League was formed in the 1920s and in 1932 the Glasgow dockers broke away from the recently merged Transport and General Workers Union to form their own Scottish organization. It was only in 1940, under stress of war, that Glasgow dockers were registered by order of the Ministry of Labour.

The National Dock Labour Scheme was formed in 1947, giving extensive protection to workers in all the main ports. This did not stop

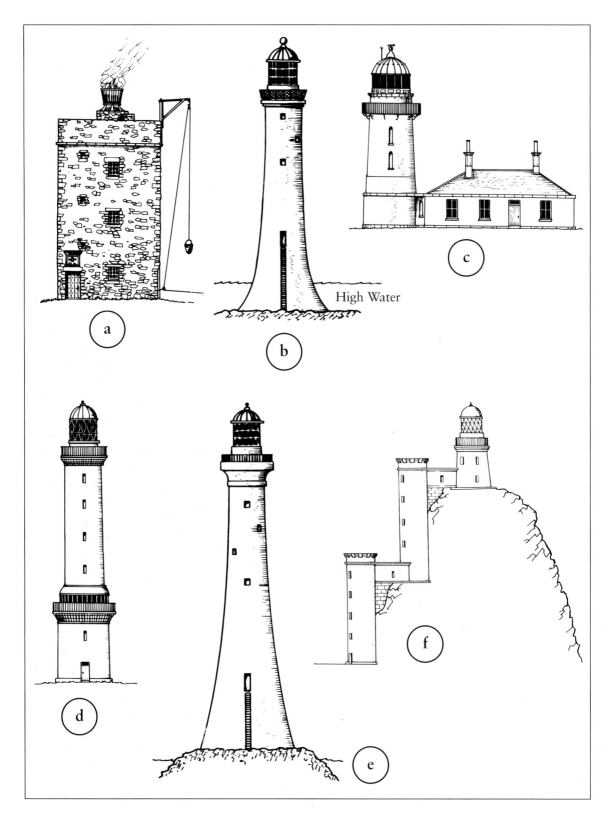

High Water

42 Some Scottish lighthouses, showing their relative heights above high-water level. In some cases this is augmented by the cliff, rock or headland on which they stand.

a. Isle of May, the first light, set up with a coal fire in 1636 and superseded in 1816.

b. The famous Bell Rock lighthouse, completed by Robert Stevenson in 1811.

c. The Toward Point lighthouse, also built in 1811.

d. Girdle Ness, built in 1833.

e. The Skerryvore light of 1844.

f. The light on the Isle of Sanda, built in 1850, with a unique staircase leading up the rocks.

a wave of militancy between 1947 and 1955, but Glasgow dockers lost only 0.7 days per man year, compared with 56.7 days in London. In 1989, when the Thatcher government abolished the National Dock Labour Scheme, there was a national strike, but support in Scotland was lukewarm. By this time containerization, the decline of the coastal trades and the move of traffic to England had devastated the Scottish labour force. Glasgow had only 60 registered dockers, Aberdeen 92 and Greenock 48.

Improving the navigation

Lighthouses are among the most dramatic and evocative monuments of maritime enterprise. This is particularly true in Scotland, where they were built with great difficulty on cliff tops, headlands, islands and rocks. This, and the activities of a remarkable family of engineers, put Scotland in the forefront of lighthouse building in the nineteenth century. The first light in Scotland was erected on the Isle of May in 1636, using a coal-fired brazier and financed by tolls on shipping (42).

Robert Stevenson (1772–1850), grandfather of Robert Louis Stevenson the Victorian novelist, was the founder of a dynasty of engineers for the Northern Lighthouse Board. His greatest achievement was the Bell Rock lighthouse, built in 1811 on a site already known as dangerous in the Middle Ages and marked by a bell buoy by the Abbot of Aberbrothock. According to Robert Southey's poem 'The Inchcape Rock':

'As a buoy in the waves it floated and swung/And over the waves its warning rung.'

Walter Scott described Stevenson's new lighthouse during a visit in 1814:

'Its dimensions are well known: but no description can give the idea of this slight, solitary round tower, trembling amid the billows. ... The fitting up within is not only handsome, but elegant. All work of wood (almost) is wainscot; all hammer work brass. You enter by a ladder of rope, with wooden steps, about thirty feet [9.1 m] of rope from the bottom, where the mason-work ceases to be solid, and admits of round apartments.'

But Bell Rock was to be succeeded by Skerryvore as the engineering marvel of the age. When Scott visited the area during the same trip, the crew and passengers of the Lighthouse Board yacht, apart from Stevenson himself, were terrified of the approach. 'There appear to be a few low broad rocks at one end of the reef, which is about a mile in length. These are never entirely under water, though the surf dashed over them.' After landing with Stevenson, Scott wrote, 'It will be a most desolate position for a lighthouse – the Bell Rock and Eddystone but a joke to it'. The Skerryvore light was eventually completed in 1844 by Alan Stevenson, son of Robert, at a cost of £86,977.

Lighthouses on headlands are just as important in navigation and far more familiar to the general public. The Cloch, built in 1797, is seen by all travellers on the Clyde, by land and sea. The great tower at Ardnamurchan Point, built by Alan Stevenson in 1849, is on the most westerly point on the British mainland. North Unst, the most northerly light in Britain, was first built in 26 days in 1854 at the request of the Admiralty to aid the British fleet during the Crimean War with Russia, though it was later replaced by a more permanent structure.

As well as their civil engineering work, the Stevensons also contributed to the illumination of lighthouses. Beginning in 1869, they began to develop a 'hyperradiant' lens which concentrated the power of a gas-burning light so that

43 Kinnaird Head lighthouse, now owned by Historic Scotland.

it could be seen many miles away.

The life of the lighthouse keeper, especially on a rock lighthouse such as Skerryvore, was traditionally a lonely one. Such posts are now extinct in the days of automation. Some lighthouses, such as Kinnaird Head in Fraserburgh, have been taken out of service and there is doubt about the future of others (43).

Specialized ports

Since the 1960s the trend has been for ports, or at least terminals within them, to specialize in a particular form of cargo, such as iron ore, oil or standardized cargo containers. The first cranes in the United Kingdom designed to handle containers came into use at Grangemouth in May 1966, but despite this early lead, container traffic is mainly with Europe and the Far East and ports in southern England have a great advantage. Greenock set up its container terminal soon afterwards, filling the old Albert Harbour, but lost its last regular customer, Hapag Lloyd, in 1987. Grangemouth has some container traffic, but is not in the top ten British container ports (colour plate 5).

Elsewhere in Scotland the oil industry is of course of paramount importance. Sullom Voe in Shetland ships more oil than any other port in Britain, 39 million tons in 1993, and in that respect it is the fourth largest port in the United Kingdom, while Aberdeen and Peterhead support the oil industry.

Ferry ports vary in scale, from tiny island ports such as Scalasaig on Colonsay, which has three services per week from Oban, to Stranraer which, along with nearby Cairnryan provides up to 13 ship and hydrofoil services per day to Northern Ireland. Yachting thrives on the west coast, with several purpose-built marinas in the Clyde area and numerous anchorages in the Highlands and Islands. Scottish harbours have changed in nature, but in many cases they are as dynamic as ever.

1. (Top) The Govan ferry waits for a steamboat to pass, c1850, in a painting by William Simpson.

2. (Left) The Lang Dyke, as seen from Dumbarton Castle at low water.

3. (Top left) The Customs House at Greenock, painted by Robert Salmon around 1820.

4. (Top right) The Broomielaw around 1840, crowded with shipping.

5. (Bottom left) Grangemouth from the air showing its origins as the mouth of the Forth and Clyde Canal. The cranes and container park of the container port are round the rectangular basin in the centre and the tanks of the oil terminal are on both sides of the channel.

6. (Bottom right) HMS *Unicorn* was built at Chatham in 1824 as a 46-gun frigate but never served at sea. In 1873 she was towed to Dundee to become the drill-ship for the Royal Naval Reserve. She served in that role until 1968 and is now preserved in Camperdown Dock.

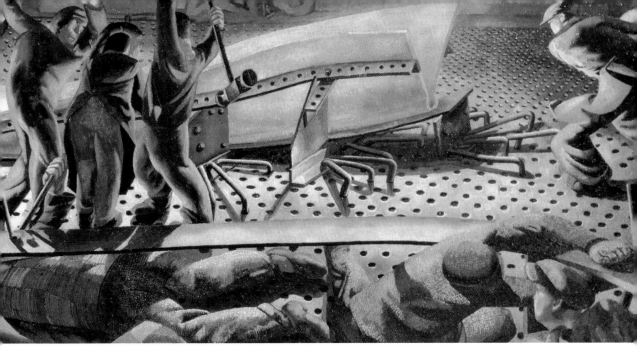

7. (Top) Bending the keel plate, a detail from a painting by Stanley Spencer, who worked as a war artist in Lithgow's Kingston Yard in Port Glasgow.

8. (Left) Kvaerner's of Govan, occupying the old Fairfield site. The bow section of a gas tanker under construction in a shed.

9. (Right) The entrance to the offices at the Fairfield Yard.

10. (Left) The Churchill Barriers from the air, looking south over the small island of Glims Holm towards Burray.

11. (Top) The engine of the *Leven* of 1824 at Dumbarton – the first steamer built by Robert Napier.

12. The Italian Chapel at Scapa Flow.

4

Resources from the Sea

Early fishing

Fish has always been important in the Scottish diet, from the people who threw their refuse on the shell mounds of Oronsay about 5500 years ago, to the twentieth-century city dweller's fish supper. In 1578 Bishop Leslie noted the variety of types of fish caught, while travellers remarked on the abundance and cheapness of fish in Scotland. It was one of pre-industrial Scotland's few exports and in 1471 Parliament encouraged burghs to build boats 'witht nettis ... for fyschinge', leading hopefully to a 'gret encress of riches to be brocht within the realme of uther cuntreis'. At Newhaven, near Edinburgh, a Society of Free Fishermen was founded in 1572, perhaps on a Flemish model. Its members fished for haddock and cod to supply Edinburgh.

In the last 200 years, Scottish fisheries have gone beyond a resource for the native population and become a major source of exports. The range of fish caught, however, has narrowed since medieval times. Shellfish became less important in the economy, except for those found in the Firth of Forth and sold in Edinburgh, or from the north-east which were used as bait in line fishing. Scottish salmon are world-famous, of course, but are from the rivers rather than the sea. The main fisheries have concentrated on two types of fish: white fish, especially haddock, cod and ling, largely caught for home consumption; and herring, pelagic or surface feeding fish, mainly for export.

Encouragement for fishing

Fishermen are noted for their individualism and contempt of authority, but the industry has always tended to attract interest from national governments. Fishing has always involved issues of state territory, as rights round the coast have to be enforced and foreigners kept out. Until well into the eighteenth century the Dutch dominated the herring fisheries and a popular print proclaimed, 'Lords of the sea to be we vainly boast, if others boldly fish upon our coasts'. In the past it was also believed that fishing would increase the supply of seamen for the Royal Navy. Furthermore, the industry needed guarantees of quality of the product, for example in official branding of herring barrels, a practice which continued even in days of laissez-faire in the late nineteenth century.

In 1749 a group of merchants pointed out the advantages of support for the herring fishery to the House of Commons: 'the civilising of His Majesty's highland subjects, the increasing of the vent of our staple manufacturers, the multiplying of seamen, the employing of a vast number of the industrious and otherwise helpless poor, lessening the parochial incumbrances, easing the public taxes, and improving the national wealth'. As a result, a system of Bounties was set up, much criticized by Adam Smith, 'It has ... been too common for vessels to fit out for the sole purpose of catching, not the fish, but the Bounty'. There was much truth in this, though he took his statistics from the year 1759, in which the trade was at its

44 The herring buss fishery off Shetland in the mid-eighteenth century, showing busses shooting nets.

worst. The problem was partly addressed by a new Act of 1786, which reduced the Bounty per boat and offered 1 shilling (5p) per barrel of cured herring, increased to 2 shillings in 1795. By that time the Scottish herring fishery was employing an average of 3366 men and boys in 294 boats and producing 53,606 barrels per year.

Between 1785 and 1914 there were 25 separate reports on the fishing industry. One of 1860 vindicated trawling against a charge of wasting fish stocks and recommended that all boats should bear a letter and number. This was enforced by an Act of 1868. Each vessel took its letters (usually the first and last letters of the port) from the local Custom House and was allocated a number within the port. In 1882 the Fishery Board for Scotland was given increased responsibilities and a research station was established at St Andrews.

Philanthropic and patriotic societies also took a keen interest in fishing. Most notable of these was the British Fisheries Society, which was founded in London in 1786 with the aim of 'erecting Free Towns, Villages and Fishing Stations, in the Highlands and Islands of Scotland, as the most effectual means of improving the Fisheries, Agriculture, Manufactures and other useful branches of Industry there'. As with Parliament in 1749, it was hoped that the problems after Culloden could be solved by investment in fishing. New towns and harbours were built at Lochbroom, Tobermory and Ullapool, but they were not ultimately successful, as the herring shoals moved away from the west coast. The east coast settlement of Pultneytown, near Wick, was of far greater importance.

The early days of the herring fishery

For most of the eighteenth century, the most favoured method of catching herring was in a relatively large boat of Dutch origin called a 'buss' (44). They were of up to 80 tons, with a large crew which was fixed by government regulations for the payment of the cash Bounty: a 47 ton buss had 11 men and a 70 ton buss had

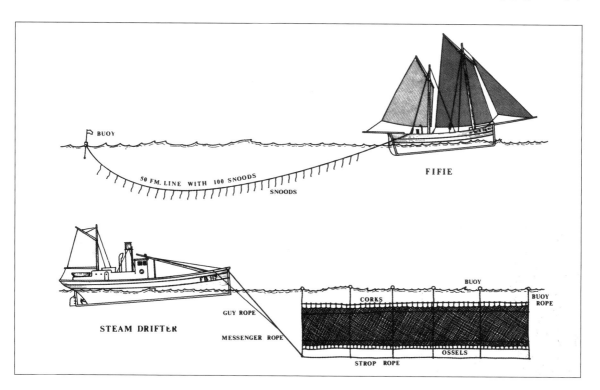

BUOY

50 FM. LINE WITH 100 SNOODS

SNOODS

FIFIE

STEAM DRIFTER

GUY ROPE

MESSENGER ROPE

STROP ROPE

CORKS

BUOY

BUOY ROPE

OSSELS

45 Line fishing (top), drift net fishing (bottom).

16. They generally fished in pairs and stayed at sea for several weeks, curing the fish on board. The Bounty system helped finance such boats, which might cost several hundred pounds to build and fit out.

Busses used drift nets, as described in 1785, 'The drift net floats with the tide and presents a perpendicular wall of netting frequently 1½ miles long and 10 yards deep. The herrings meeting this net mesh themselves into it and being caught either by the gill covers or by the body, are hanged and die'. The method remained standard until the second half of the twentieth century (45).

Fish, especially herring, decay very quickly after death. This was acceptable for Newhaven fish sold in Edinburgh, or Loch Fyne herring sold in Glasgow: but if they were to serve anything beyond a purely local market, means had to be found to preserve them for weeks or months: the technique of curing herring was the great secret which had kept the Dutch in the forefront of the trade since the sixteenth century.

In Scotland, local methods of curing developed in different communities, giving brands which retain their identity to this day. Most involved gutting the fish or cutting it open and then smoking over a fire. At Findon, each fish was split open and smoked over a fire.

Because of the unpredictable movements of the herring shoals, the first Scottish herring boom occurred in Caithness in the 1790s, largely independent of government support (46). Though the Bounty proved useful, it was not the large, decked busses which made the difference, but small local craft bringing their fish ashore for curing. Local tradesmen entered the curing business, preparing the fish for export to the West Indies and the cities to the south, while fishermen from the other side of the Moray Firth arrived during the season. The harbour at Wick became excessively crowded as the number of boats leapt from 214 in 1808 to 822 in 1814.

The success of Caithness inspired other fishermen on the east coast to follow their example, often sending boats north during July to September. Since herring move in shoals, the

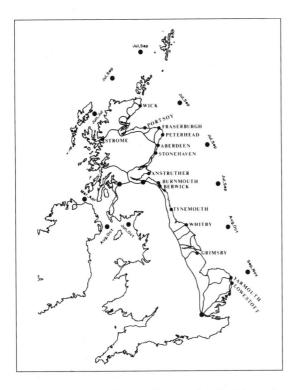

46 The movements of the herring shoals round the Scottish coast in 1882, showing the main fishing ports and rail links.

trade could be erratic – no fish at all for days or weeks and then perhaps a bumper catch in one night.

In the *New Statistical Account of Scotland*, published in 1845, the minister of Dunbeath gives a description of fishing at the time:

'The boats usually leave the shore from 5 to 7 o'clock in the afternoon, according to the direction of the wind and the distance at which the fish are supposed to be found, and shoot their nets about dusk. In this state they remain, with the boat attached to each drift by means of a head rope, and slowly carried east or west by the tide, until about 3 o'clock the next morning. Then all hands are employed in the hauling of the nets and fish at the boat's stern, while they remain together dispersed over the boat, till it comes to shore, when they commence the operation of disengaging the fish from the meshes of the net.'

The Shetlanders had watched the Dutch exploit the herring off their coasts for many

decades, without the finance to create a buss fishery of their own. Instead they concentrated on the 'haaf' fishery, in which crofter-fishermen used four-oared 'foureens' in long-line fishing for cod and ling, curing the catch in small bays known as 'haaf-stations'. By the late 1830s, Shetlanders were learning from Caithness, adopting the scaffie as the main type of boat and taking part in the herring fishery on a large scale.

White fish

White fish consists mainly of haddock and cod, along with ling, skate, halibut and turbot. These are 'demersal' or bottom feeding fish, so the methods of catching them were different from those used for herring. They were caught mainly for local and national markets, not for export, so they attracted less government interest than the herring. In the late nineteenth century, fish and chips became a central feature of the industrial diet.

Haddock was generally caught inshore using lines carrying 800 to 1000 hooks, attached to short lines known as 'snoods', 14 in (0.3 m) long and 30 in (0.7 m) apart, baited with mussels or lugworms. Cod was caught further from land, by bigger boats which used 'great lines'. These had larger hooks, about 120 to a line, with snoods 5 ft (1.5 m) long and 15 ft (4.5 m) apart, baited with small haddock and herring.

The trawl net, which could be hauled over the bottom of the sea to catch demersal fish such as cod and haddock, was an English invention which slowly spread throughout the North Sea during the nineteenth century (47). The Scots were deeply suspicious of it, and never adopted the sailing trawler. However, the steam trawler, introduced in England in the 1880s, had the great advantage that fishing could continue even when the winds were light. The first steam trawlers began to appear in Scottish waters in 1880s, and the Scots were forced to adopt it for themselves. However the main estuaries, the Forth, Moray Firth and other inshore waters were closed to trawling in

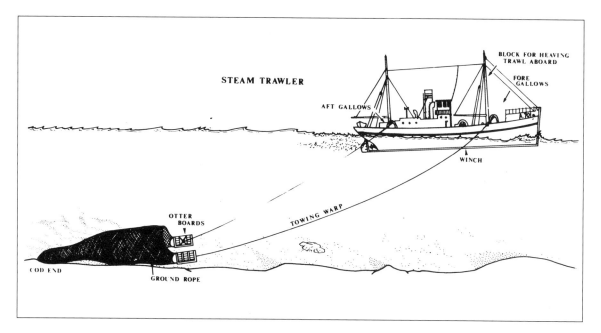

STEAM TRAWLER

BLOCK FOR HEAVING
TRAWL ABOARD

FORE
GALLOWS

AFT GALLOWS

WINCH

OTTER
BOARDS

TOWING WARP

COD END

GROUND ROPE

47 Trawling.

a series of regulations passed between 1885 and 1892. By 1905, 1,745,000 cwt (88,000,000 kg) of fish landed in Scotland were caught in trawls, compared with only 735,000 cwt (37,000,000 kg) caught by lines.

The golden age of the herring fishery

Scottish herring developed an almost limitless export market during the nineteenth century, to Ireland and the West Indies in the first instance. After the abolition of slavery and the Irish Famine destroyed these markets, fish were sold in vast quantities in Germany and Russia.

The herring fishermen of the Firth of Clyde operated in a different environment from those in the West Highlands or the east coast. They worked in relatively sheltered waters, especially on Loch Fyne, with small boats serving the local market in industrial Clydeside, selling fresh fish without the need for curing. In the eighteenth century the industry was based at Greenock, Rothesay and Campbeltown and used drift nets like other herring fishermen. In the mid 1830s, the men of Tarbert began to surround the shoals with drift nets and soon began to develop a technique of 'ring netting'

(sometimes improperly known as trawling). This was fiercely resisted by other fishermen, leading to violent disputes and even deaths in conflict with naval patrols. It was outlawed between 1851 and 1867, but finally became the standard method of fishing in the area. In 1883 there were 431 boats operating on Kilbrannan Sound between Arran and Kintyre and 261 in Loch Fyne, mostly ring-netters. They were served by up to 20 steamers which carried the fish to market.

At the peak in 1890, approximately 100,000 people were employed in the Scottish fisheries, just under half on the boats themselves. After that the numbers declined slowly, though catches increased due to improved efficiency. In 1913 90,000 Scots were employed directly in fishing, including 38,000 on the boats themselves, 16,000 as gutters and packers and the rest in the carrying trade and ancillary activities. Aberdeen alone landed more than 2 million tons of fish.

Other resources

Salt pans provided a ready market for the growing coal industry, and the product was essential in preserving fish. High duties on imported salt had been imposed at the Union

48 The windmill used to pump water into the salt pans at St Monance, Fife.

of 1707 and the Scottish industry was prosperous, selling its surplus in northern England. They were common on the Firth of Forth, with 85 in operation on the Fife side in 1719 (48). Henry Kalmeter, a Swedish visitor that year, described the operation of one at Wemyss:

'The water was raised by a windmill, into an iron pan 18 ft [5.5 m] long and 9 ft [2.7 m] wide, to a depth of 15 inches [0.3 m], smeared inside with lime. It was heated with coals and then the water was allowed in. Impurities were removed by scraping off the scum from the top and the water boiled off. The pan was filled four times during the process over a period of 36 hours.'

The kelp industry was another industry which extracted valuable goods from the sea. Around the middle of the eighteenth century it was found that certain kinds of seaweed such as kelp could produce alkali, essential for bleaching in the Scottish linen industry. The seaweed had to be harvested at low tide in the summer, then 'calcined' by burning at a constant temperature in a peat fire. The industry boomed during the Napoleonic Wars up to 1815, because alternative sources of alkali were cut off, but slumped soon afterwards. It left few physical traces, except that it helped to create the subdivisions of land which soon became known as 'crofts'.

Fishing ports

Around 1800, Scottish fishing was conducted from numerous tiny ports – in the north-east, from Findhorn to Montrose, there were 70 communities, one every 2 miles. Many were just open beaches where boats could be hauled

49 Wick Harbour in 1875, with hundreds of fishing boats and women gutting and packing in the foreground.

50 Thomas Telford's plan for the village and harbour of Pultneytown, near Wick, in 1807.

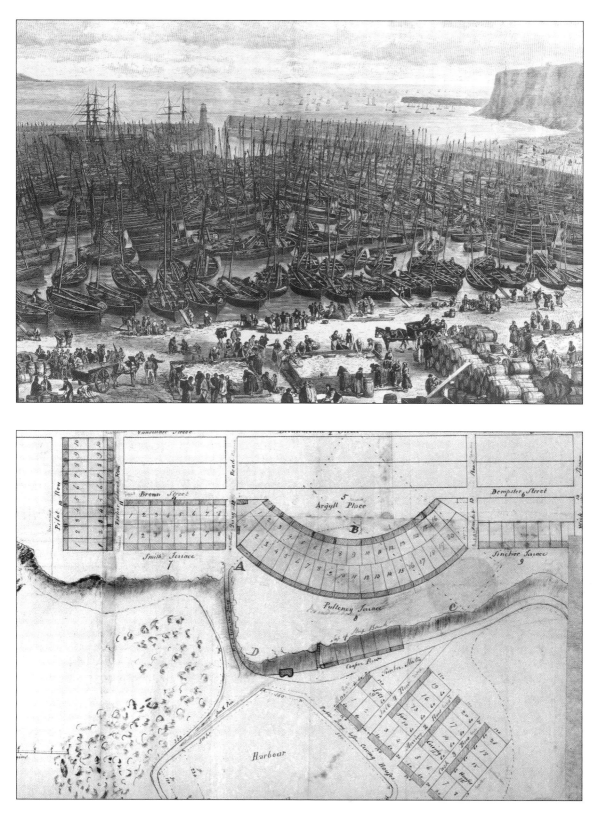

up. Simple cottages huddled round the harbour, often separate, geographically and culturally, from a nearby town. Though a beach, especially of shingle, was adequate as a harbour, it was not a place to build houses and the fishermen often had to live some distance away, perhaps at the top of a cliff. The most extreme example was at Whaligoe in Caithness, where 365 steps lead down to the shore. In the middle of the nineteenth century, Whaligoe was used by 35 boats and 140 fishermen.

The lack of suitable ports, especially on the east coast, became a drag on the Scottish fishing industry by the middle of the nineteenth century. As a local minister reported of Caithness in 1845:

'Considering the vast importance of this coast in a commercial point of view, the great number of vessels that frequent it in connection with the fisheries, and the many risks to which life and property are exposed in consequence of its bold, rocky, and exposed character, it is much to be regretted that so little has hitherto been done in order to obtain safe and commodious harbours.' (49)

As well as the works undertaken by the British Fisheries Society (50), many harbours were built on the initiative of the local landowners, such as the one at Cullen in Banffshire begun by the Earl of Seafield in 1817. After enlargement and the expenditure of £10,000 it was regarded in 1845 as 'one of the best harbours in the Moray Frith [sic]'. Not all efforts at improvement were successful: at Nairn, a small pier had 'been much injured by floods in the river, and an accumulation of sand driven in the sea, so as to be of little use ...'. The Fishery Board, set up by the national government in 1809, turned its attention to harbour improvement after 1828. It too had its failures, at Sarclet in Caithness and Dunbar for example, but over 85 years it built or improved many piers and harbours all round the coast.

With the rise of trawling, bigger and much more sophisticated ships demanded bigger harbours with much better facilities. This type of fishing soon became concentrated on Aberdeen and Peterhead. At the former port a new fish market was opened in 1889 but was still inadequate and had to be enlarged twice.

The fisher girls

Though women never went to sea in fishing boats, they have always played an essential role in fishing communities. In remote villages, they baited the lines and cured the catch. According to a report in the Old Statistical Account of Scotland in the 1790s:

'The fisher wives lead a most laborious life. They assist in dragging the boats on the beach, and in launching them. They sometimes, in frosty weather, and at unseasonable hours, carry their husbands on board, to keep them dry. They receive the fish from the boats, carry them, fresh or after salting, to their customers and to market.'

51 Scottish fishery girls working at Scarborough, Yorkshire, c 1900

In the pre-industrial fisheries, fishwives sold the catches, especially at Newhaven which served the large Edinburgh market. They gained a proverbial reputation as quarrelsome and noisy. A very different picture, however, was painted by the Edinburgh actress Fanny Kemble of Mrs Sandie Flockhart of Newhaven around 1828. She was:

'one of the very handsomest [women] I ever saw, ... tall as well as large, and her grey-green eyes might have become Venus Anadyomene herself, turned into a Scotch fishwife of five-and-thirty. ... She was a splendid specimen of her tribe, climbing the steep Edinburgh streets with her bare white feet, the heavy fish-basket at her back, hardly stooping her broad shoulders, her florid face sheltered, ... and her still, sweet voice calling "caller haddie".'

By the end of the nineteenth century women had taken on a more specialized but equally demanding role in the new industrial fisheries. They moved around the east coast of Scotland and England working as gutters and packers, invading the East Anglian ports of Yarmouth and Lowestoft in September and October, making the same trip by land as their local men and boats did by sea (51). Others found work in fish processing plants or net-making factories as the trade became more specialized and industrial.

Hazards of the sea

Fishing has always been a particularly dangerous occupation, even by the standards of seafarers in the age of sail. With the great expansion of the fishing fleet in the early nineteenth century, large casualty figures began to attract public attention. In August 1848, 900 boats from Wick and Peterhead were caught in a storm but the water was too low to let them enter Wick Harbour. One hundred and twenty-four boats were lost on the coast and 100 men died. The worst local disaster occurred at Eyemouth in October 1881, when 129 men from that village alone were lost, together with 62 from other parts of the coast. In the same year, 58 men were lost in a storm off Shetland.

Three hundred out of 1500 trawlers registered in Aberdeen were lost from various causes, including enemy action.

In theory, modern fishing boats are much safer, with powerful engines, weather forecasting and radio distress signals, but disasters still occur from year to year and often strike a chord with the public imagination. The twentieth century introduced a new hazard to fishing boats, especially in the Clyde – the submarine. In 1990 the *Antares* of Carradale caught her nets in a submarine and was dragged down with the loss of her crew of four. At first the Royal Navy refused to confirm whether submarines were in the area, but the incident led to broadcast warnings of submarine operations.

Fishing boats under oars and sail

The shape of Scottish fishing boats had probably changed little over the centuries, when Captain Washington produced a report on the Wick disaster of 1848 and provided details of many local types. Most showed clear traces of Viking origin, especially the 'yoles' of Orkney and the foureens and sixareens of Shetland, which retained the shape of small Norse craft and were often prefabricated from parts sent over from Norway (52). Most other types were clinker-built and had a pointed or round stern, for the flat transom stern favoured in southern England was almost unknown.

Few, however, were completely double-ended, as in the original Viking craft, because the stern rudder was universal. Some, such as the Oban skiff, had a sharp bow and a beautifully rounded stern. Others, such as the 'scaffie' of the Moray Firth, had straight, angled stern post and a curved stempost (53), while the 'Fifie', which of course originated in Fife, had an almost vertical stem and stern posts above water, though they were curved underwater (54). Over the next few decades, the Fifie bow and stern developed until they became more angular underwater.

Until the second half of the nineteenth century, Scottish fishermen were very reluctant to

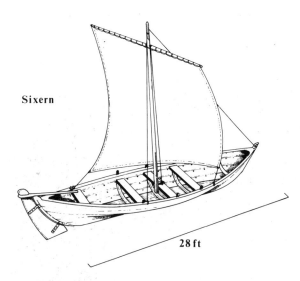

Sixern

28 ft

52 A Shetland Sixern, obviously descended from Viking boats.

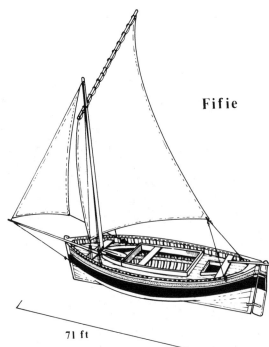

Fifie

71 ft

54 The Fifie *True Vine* of Methil, Fife.

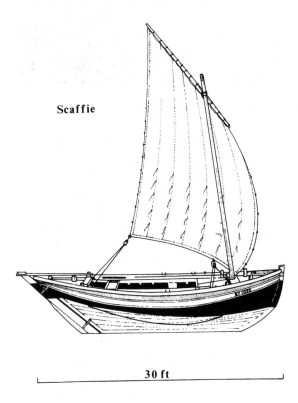

Scaffie

30 ft

53 A Scaffie, *Mary Ann* , of 1848

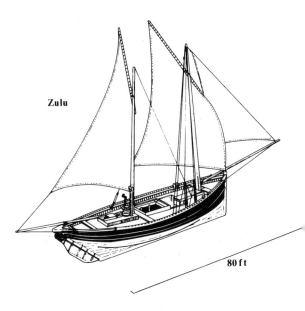

Zulu

80 ft

55 A Zulu, the *Muirneag*, built at Buckie in 1903. (These four drawings based on models in the National Maritime Museum.)

56 An undecked drifter loaded with fish at Wick, c. 1880.

build decks on their boats. They would be obliged to work on an exposed deck rather than in the shelter of the inside of the vessel, while decks were less necessary on boats which rarely spent more than 24 hours away from the home port, or from a beach where tents might be pitched (56). Against this, a decked boat provided shelter for the off-duty crew and was less likely to be swamped in bad weather. As boats got bigger in the middle of the century, decks began to seem more desirable. Eyemouth built its first decked boat in 1856 and 18 years later, 40 full-decked boats were used in the district; but change was slow, and the majority of east coast boats were open or half-decked until late in the nineteenth century.

The scaffie was a very efficient boat while fishermen stayed in inshore waters, but in heavy seas it was said that 'tested by the conditions under which the boats of the Fifie model show to advantage, the Scaffie is rather a dangerous craft, owing to the extent to which its stem and stern project beyond the respective extremities of the keel'. The Fifie, on the other hand, was too stable and difficult to tack because of its great keel length. A compromise was produced in 1879, the year of the Zulu wars in South Africa. According to reports it was designed by a Lossiemouth fisherman, 'Dad' Campbell, after a disagreement with his wife about the best type. The new 'zulu' used the straight bow of the Fifie and the raked stern of the scaffie, to produce a type which was one of the most successful of the age (55).

Whaling

Scotland was clearly well situated for the northern whale fishery, in which Greenland right whales, up to 60 ft (18.3 m) long, were caught in the Greenland Sea and Davis Strait, north of the Arctic circle. But whaling required much capital and Scottish participation was very limited until 1750, when the government Bounty was increased from 30 shillings (£1.50) per ton to £2. A ship of 333 tons, financed by the Whale-fishing Company of Edinburgh, set

57 The Greenland whale fishery as depicted by Charles Brooking and John Boydell in 1754.

out but returned 'clean', having caught no whales. The following year was even less successful, and one of the two ships sent out was lost. In 1752, three ships were reasonably successful and in the following year, 14 Scottish ships went to the Arctic from the Forth ports of Leith and Bo'ness. By 1814, despite the difficulties caused by a long war with France, 48 Scottish ships produced 6383 tons of oil, about a third of the British total (57).

Whale oil was of great importance for lighting and many other purposes. Whalebone, from the skin lining the mouth of the whale, was useful for many articles that today would be made of plastic, for example ladies' corsets. The whales were caught using harpoons thrown by hand by a skilled harpooner mounted in a boat launched from the parent ship. After being hit, the whale was likely to dive for 30 to 40 minutes and the whale-boat carried 720 ft (219.5 m) of line to keep in contact and

could join lines if necessary. When the creature surfaced again, other boats from the ship were waiting to complete the kill and up to eight hits might be needed. After killing, the whale was brought alongside the ship where it was cut apart or 'flensed', causing the crew to work hard in revolting conditions. The blubber was then boiled in a furnace known as the 'try-works' and stored in barrels in the hold.

At Lerwick, both Scottish and English ships anchored and made up their crews from the native population. Walter Scott observed their behaviour in 1814:

'The streets full of drunken riotous sailors from the whale-vessels. It seems these ships take about 1000 sailors from Zetland every year. ... These Zetlanders, as they get a part of their pay on landing, make a point of treating

58 Some details of a Scottish steam whaler, c. 1900, showing boats with harpoon guns and methods of towing and lifting the carcass.

their English messmates, who get drunk of course, and are very riotous. The Zetlanders themselves do not get drunk, but go straight home to their houses...'

Despite the considerable economic importance of whaling, the eighteenth- and nineteenth-century whale fisheries employed a relatively small amount of shipping, and the numbers caught were quite small. In 1763, for example, the *Cambleton* of Leith was the most successful ship in the British fleet, with 12 whales. No other Scottish ship came home with more than three. Whaling was much affected by enemy privateers in wartime and in 1783, during the American War of Independence, the fleet fell to four or five ships. After that there was a boom and 31 went out in 1788 from nine Scottish ports,

including Leith, Dunbar and even Queensferry.

Peterhead sent out its first boat that year, though it was 1799 before it began its rise to become the leading British whaling port. In 1845 it overtook Hull, while Aberdeen's effort declined to almost nothing. By 1857, Peterhead fitted out 31 ships out of a total of 55 in the British fleet, and Hull was the only English port still in the trade.

There were many dangers in whaling. The whale itself might capsize the boat in icy waters, or limbs might be lost as the harpoon line ran out under great tension. All the usual dangers of shipwreck were present, along with those of exposure. Some ships were caught in the winter ice, such as the *Advice of Dundee*, which lost 10 or 11 of her crew during the winter of 1836–7.

Peterhead's whalemen were innovative enough. They tried iron hulls in 1858, but these proved less successful than wood in the

Arctic ice. The port's supremacy was chal-
lenged in 1859 when the *Narwhal*, the first
whaler with an auxiliary steam engine, was
built by Alexander Stephens for a Dundee company (58). Sixteen more were built in Dundee
in the next 25 years, and by that time Dundee
had left Peterhead behind, with 15 ships, compared with Peterhead's five in 1881. But the
Arctic whaling industry was about to enter a
crisis with falling prices due to Norwegian
competition, then the near extinction of the
species.

In these circumstances, the firm of Christian
Salvesen of Leith found new whaling waters in
the south Atlantic and developed new techniques to catch the whales. Salvesen adopted the
explosive harpoon and steam whale-catcher
developed by his Norwegian countrymen. In
1907 he sent his first expedition south, consis-
ting of four 80 ft (24.4 m) boats with 120 horsepower engines and harpoon guns mounted in
the bows. Such small vessels could not operate
alone for long and had no facilities for flensing.
The port of Leith Harbour, on the island of
South Georgia, was developed as a base.
Salvesen also employed factory ships to process
the carcasses, beginning in 1911–12 when two
cargo ships were converted. Up to 16 whale-
catchers would be used in future years.

Whaling, once a contest between man and
the greatest creatures on earth, was becoming
an organised mass slaughter – Salvesen alone
caught 2350 whales in 1911–12. The new techniques, like all modern methods of fishing, led
to increased regulation. Salvesen gave up whaling in 1963, before public opinion turned deci-
sively against it.

Fishing boats under power

Steam boats had long been used in the Clyde to
carry catches to market, but the steam trawlers
were the first boats to use power for catching
fish. They had evolved on the English east
coast before the first Scottish boats were built
in Aberdeen in the 1880s. Steam power came
slightly later in drifters (59). It was not used in
the actual fishing, but it was useful in leaving

59 A steam drifter, the *Accumulator*, of 1955.

60 A seine netter of the late 1960s, with wooden construction and
traditional shape, but with a short shelter deck in the bows.

61 A boat of the late 1980s with metal construction, a transom
stern and a long shelter deck.

and returning to harbour in unfavourable winds. By 1914 it was standard. The typical boat was about 90 ft (27.4 m) long and 18 ft 6 in (5.6 m) broad, with two masts, the aftermost of which could carry a small sail to steady the boat and turn its head to wind while the nets were out. The boat was divided into watertight compartments and used acetylene gas for lighting. It had a compound steam engine which could drive it at 10 or 11 knots and it cost £3500 to £4000 to build.

Since the late 1920s, drifters have tended to adopt the cruiser stern, rounded in both the horizontal and vertical plane (60). In 1964 the first boat with a square or transom stern was built, offering greater space for the handling of tackle, and this soon became the norm. In the next decade it became common to cover part of the deck with a 'gutting shelter' made of glass, reinforced plastic or aluminium, where the crew could work in more comfort. Rope storage reels were introduced to reduce the labour in handling lines, while the wheelhouse, traditionally in the stern, was placed in midships or forward on some boats (61). There was a much greater variety in shape and fittings as skippers and owners were allowed more choice about layout, while the market for boats became more international and the purely Scottish identity began to decline. Diesel power has been used increasingly since the 1920s, as it is more economical of fuel and needs less maintenance than steam.

Fishing in the modern world

The Scottish fishing industry suffered heavily during both world wars. Many boats and crews were taken away for minesweeping or naval harbour duties, while the great markets for herring, in Germany and Russia, were cut off and were never to recover.

Since 1945, fishing methods have become increasingly sophisticated. Navigation has been made easier by such devices as Decca and Satnav. Sonar has been used more and more, in the form of a 'fishfinder' to detect shoals. Even more dramatically, drifting has been made

completely obsolete since the 1960s by the use of the purse seine net, in which the shoal is surrounded rather in the manner of the ring-net of the Clyde, or the mid-water trawl which can be hauled near the surface of the water rather than the bottom by two boats 'pair trawling'.

In view of all this technological progress, the main concern has been to conserve fish stocks in the face of over-fishing. It is not a new problem – trawling bans were instituted in the 1880s in inshore areas – but the scale is much greater than ever. Between 1958 and 1976 Britain had three 'Cod wars' when Iceland tried, with ultimate success, to extend her territorial waters to 12, 50 and then 200 miles. Britain's entry to the European Economic Community (as it then was) in 1973 had compounded the problem, opening British waters to a certain amount of 'quota-hopping' by foreign vessels, while regulation from Brussels has seemed remote and inimical to British interests. At the same time, eastern European 'Klondykers' have fished extensively outside territorial waters, basing their factory ships in Lerwick and other Scottish ports.

Despite its relative decline in the European market, fishing attracts much public and media attention. The fisherman, the last hunter-gatherer in an over-controlled world, still seems heroic. As John Grierson wrote of his famous documentary *Drifters* in 1929:

'Two miles of nets to every ship, hand over hand agonies of eight hours on end, a dash for harbour in heavy seas, the long labour of unshipping the catch at whatever hour of day or darkness the boat arrives, putting out again, shooting, hauling, seven days out of seven. ... It is its own story – an adventure story in a ready-made sequence of dramatics.'

It has attracted the attention of all the major Scottish poets of the twentieth century. As Norman McCaig wrote in 1955:

'The long net, tasselled with corpses, came
Burning through the water, flowing up.
Dogfish following it to the surface
Turned away slowly to the deep.'

The oil industry

In 1964, the British government reached agreement with other nations on the division of the resources of the North Sea and issued the first licenses to explore for oil and gas. The Forties Field, 100 miles west of Aberdeen, was discovered by British Petroleum in 1970. The Oil Crisis of 1973–4 put North Sea oil at the forefront of economic development. It quadrupled the price of oil and drew attention to the fact that, despite the expense of finding and extracting it, North Sea oil was to be found in a relatively stable part of the world.

Oil exploration and extraction from the sea demanded a whole range of rigs or platforms, to be used in different conditions: rigs for deep or shallow water, moveable rigs for exploration, permanent rigs for extraction of a large field (62). Drill-ships use 'dynamic positioning' to keep their station in rough seas. Semi-submersibles, such as those used in the Balmoral and Glamis fields, are floating production platforms. Steel and concrete platforms, such as the Brent Spar whose scrapping caused great controversy in 1996, are used in water of medium depth. Jack-up rigs are relatively mobile and can be used in shallow waters.

Very little of this technology is ever seen by the general public. Oil platforms are nearly all situated a long way offshore, in a sea that is little used by leisure and passenger craft. The names of the fields are a combination of the exotic and the commonplace, caused by the naming policies of the different companies – Tiffany and Thelma, Ivanhoe and Rob Roy, Cyprus and Tommeliten. Scottish shipyards have played some part in the construction of the equipment, but had only a small share of the work in the early stages. Yards were set up at Ardyne Point opposite Rothesay and at Kishorn in Wester Ross, but have been abandoned. Rig building continues at Clydebank.

Pipe-layers and support vessels are more

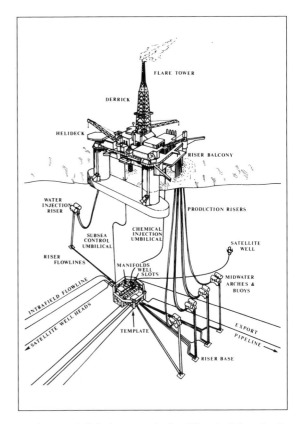

62 The type of oil platform set up by Sun Oil on the Balmoral and Glamis fields in 1986–9.

likely to be seen as they visit the main oil ports, such as Aberdeen and Peterhead. The oil itself is mainly pumped ashore through pipelines to Nigg Bay, St Fergus and Cruden Bay. It eventually reaches refineries such as that of BP at Grangemouth. Oil from the most northerly fields, such as Piper, Claymore, Ninian and Cormorant, comes ashore at Orkney or Shetland, where it is shipped in giant tankers from Flotta and Sullom Voe.

North Sea oil production peaked in 1986 at 120 million tonnes. It still employs around 300,000 people and is a vital factor in the Scottish economy. New exploration might soon open up new fields in the even deeper and stormier waters to the west of Shetland.

5
Shipbuilding

Before the nineteenth century, Scotland had hardly enough shipyards to supply her own, local needs and in 1695 warships for her navy had to be built in England. She built only three ships for the Royal Navy before 1815, none more than 200 tons in a period when ships of over 2000 tons were quite common. Trade with America stimulated some native shipbuilding, but Scotland was short of suitable timber. Even so two of the older firms, Scott's (founded in Greenock in 1711), and Alexander Stephens (originated in Lossiemouth in 1750), survived into the modern age to be numbered among the giants of Clyde shipbuilding. But it was only with the development of steam power and iron construction that Scottish shipbuilding came into prominence on a British and then a world scale. Until then Scottish ship design had been passive. The Scots had adopted the coracle of Columbus, the Viking longship, the Dutch trading ship and the English warship, perhaps adding touches of their own but not altering the basic design.

The steam engine was not a Scottish invention but James Watt (1736–1819), with his separate condenser and other improvements, quadrupled its efficiency. He started this work during his time as an instrument maker in Glasgow University, but he had to go to Birmingham to put his machines into production. The application of steam power to ships was projected several times throughout the eighteenth century in England, France and America. William Symington's *Charlotte*

Dundas was tried on the Forth and Clyde Canal in 1789, but not adopted for fear that its wash would damage the banks. In 1812 Henry Bell built the *Comet*, a paddle steamer of 205 tons, to carry passengers from Glasgow to his hotel in Helensburgh. It was a world milestone as the first successful commercial use of a steamship and locally it marked the discovery of the ideal way of moving in the Clyde valley.

Two cousins, David and Robert Napier, played a key role in the development of steam ships and shipbuilding over the next 60 years. Both were born in Dumbarton in 1790-1 and learned ironworking trades under their fathers. David made part of the engine for the *Comet* then set up in business at Camlachie in Glasgow, moving to Lancefield in 1814-5. He promoted steamship services on several pioneering routes, usually making the engines himself. The *Dumbarton Castle* was the first to go up Loch Fyne and the Britannia began a service down the Firth of Clyde as far as Campbeltown. He was not involved in two steamers built at Greenock for a service between Wales and Ireland, but this inspired him to build the *Rob Roy* in 1818, to ply from Glasgow to Dublin, the first regular steam service in coastal waters. He claimed to have developed a hull with a much sharper bow by a form of tank testing:

'Having obtained a block of wood of the proportional length, breadth and depth I intended to build the *Rob Roy*, ... I carefully noted the time the weight took to descend,

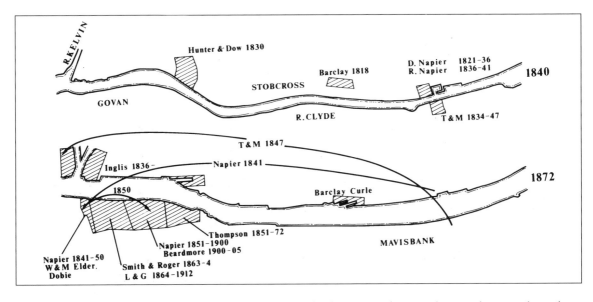

63 The first phases of Glasgow shipbuilding:

  a The situation up to 1840.

  b The first move down river.

dragging the block at the same time through the water, and continued fining the bow as long as there was any perceptible increase to the speed ... which block or model I gave to the shipbuilder to take off his lines for building the *Rob Roy*. When it was launched nautical people said I had put the wrong end foremost.'

His *United Kingdom*, built by Robert Steele at Greenock in 1826, was the largest steamship yet, 160 ft (48.8 m) long with a 200 horsepower engine. She plied between Leith and London. Napier invented the steeple engine, which was more compact than the side lever engine, important in the crowded hull of a ship. He was not the only Scottish pioneer of steam. In 1814 Cook of Tradeston, Glasgow, engined the *Thames*, which made the first passage from Glasgow to London and the *Margery*, the first to cross the English Channel.

Robert Napier was less of a genius than his cousin, but his work in building engines and ships and in training others earned him the title 'Father of Clyde Shipbuilding'. Taking over the works at Camlachie, he built his first engine, for the paddle steamer *Leven*, in 1823 (colour plate 11). Moving to Lancefield in 1836, he

built engines for ever bigger ships, such as the *British Queen* for the transatlantic run in 1839. His customers included Thomas Assheton Smith, a wealthy English yachtsman who ordered many fast steamers, such as the *Fire King* of 1839, the fastest vessel of her day.

With ships approaching the maximum size possible with wooden construction and the forests depleted of suitable timber, iron offered many advantages, but took some time to develop. The technique had originated with canal boats, mainly built in the ironworking districts of England, but the first Scottish one was the *Vulcan*, built in 1818 for the Forth and Clyde Canal. The *Aaron Manby*, built in Staffordshire in 1822, was the first iron seagoing steamship. During the 1830s Laird's of Merseyside were the leading exponents, but Brunel's *Great Britain*, begun at Bristol in 1838, was to prove the quantum leap in iron shipbuilding. She demonstrated the value of iron when she ran aground on the Irish coast in 1846. She was salvaged after a year, though a wooden ship would have broken up in hours. In 1841 Robert Napier, realising that his metalworking experience was valuable in the new craft of iron shipbuilding, opened his first shipyard at Govan.

The use of iron was one of several factors which favoured the fantastic growth of Clyde

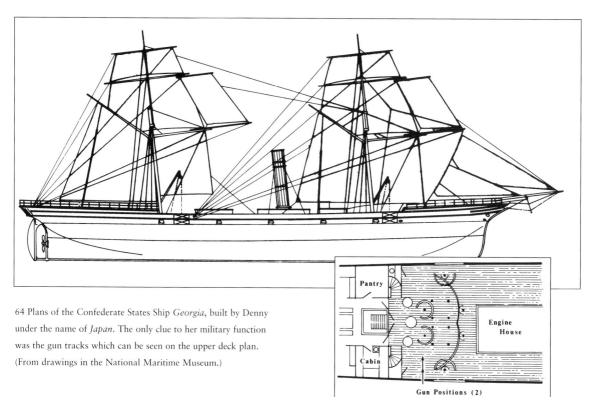

64 Plans of the Confederate States Ship *Georgia*, built by Denny under the name of *Japan*. The only clue to her military function was the gun tracks which can be seen on the upper deck plan. (From drawings in the National Maritime Museum.)

Pantry

Engine House

Cabin

Gun Positions (2)

shipbuilding in the middle of the nineteenth century. In the first instance a market was created by local needs. There had not been enough suitable timber in Scotland to supply ships for her own merchants; but the transition to iron and steel offered a new opportunity. From 1830–70, the ironmasters of Lanarkshire led the world, due partly to J B Neilson's hot-blast furnaces. After 1870, the mild steel industry in Scotland produced a material well suited to shipbuilding.

The deepening of the Clyde created firm banks fronting deep water, providing green field sites, while the river was especially suitable for the use of steam power. But local needs were not enough to create a whole river devoted to shipbuilding: a world market had to be found and exploited.

The Scottish educational tradition produced naval architects, managers and skilled workmen. The Institute of Engineers and Shipbuilders in Scotland was founded in 1857, the first regional organization of its kind. In 1883, the chair of Naval Architecture Glasgow University, the first in the country, was endowed by Mrs Isabella Elder, widow of joint inventor of the compound engine. At the same time, immigration from Ireland and the Highlands expanded the pool of cheap unskilled labour.

The growth of Clyde shipbuilding

In the 1830s and 1840s, Clyde shipbuilding began to move out of its infancy. David Tod and John McGregor left Napier's Lancefield works in 1833 and five years later set up the Clyde's first iron shipbuilding yard across the river in Mavisbank (63). In 1844 several members of an established shipbuilding family in Dumbarton set up the firm of Denny Brothers, specifically to build iron ships. William Denny had served under Robert Napier at Lancefield.

Meanwhile, older firms began to learn new techniques. Scott's of Greenock built an iron ship of 1190 tons for the transatlantic route in the early 1850s and had finished with wooden

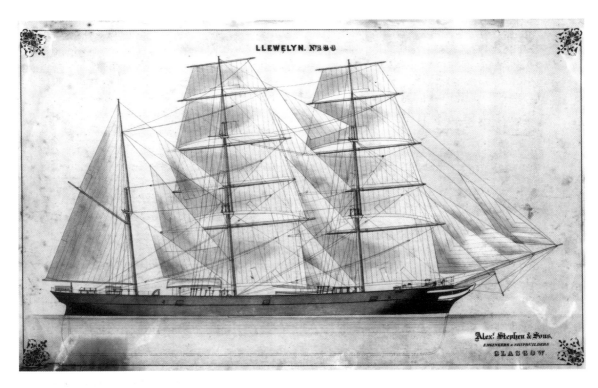

LLEWELYN. Nº 380

Alexr Stephen & Sons.
ENGINEERS & SHIPBUILDERS
GLASGOW.

construction by 1859. Alexander Stephen
arrived at Kelvinhaugh from Dundee in 1851.
His first vessel, the iron sailing ship *Typhoon*,
was launched the following year. Barclay Curle,
which had been founded by Robert Barclay at
Stobcross in 1818, built its first iron ship in
1852. By 1870 the Clyde was producing 70 per
cent of British iron tonnage.

World events favoured the growth of the new
shipbuilding industry. Monopolies such as the
East India Company were abolished, increasing
competition. Free trade, based on Adam Smith's
Wealth of Nations of 1776, became the accepted
doctrine. British manufacturing industry was at
its strongest, needing ships to export its products. The railway, far from damaging shipping,
needed steamer links with rail services. In a different vein, the southern states in the American
Civil War demanded both fast blockade runners
and commerce raiders to attack northern shipping. Denny, for example, secretly built several
ships for the Confederates, including the innocu-
ously named *Ajax* and *Hercules* for the defence
of Wilmington (64). United States shipping suffered heavily from the commerce raiders, while

65 The original rigging plan of the *Llewellyn*, built by Alexander
Stephens in 1875.

American builders, world leaders in the days of
wood, were left behind in the new techniques of
iron shipbuilding; the opening of the Suez Canal
in 1869 was a further boost for the steamship.
By 1870 more than 40 per cent of world merchant shipping was registered in Britain.

Technology in shipbuilding

It was developments in the marine engine that
led the next phase. John Elder and Charles
Randolph, who had worked with Robert
Napier, took out their first patent for a compound engine in 1853. High-pressure steam was
reused in a second cylinder, improving fuel efficiency by 40–50 per cent. In 1874 Dr A C Kirk,
one of their former employees, added another
cylinder to make the triple expansion engine.
Fuel efficiency increased yet again, in perhaps
the biggest breakthrough of all. Steam power
was no longer an auxiliary to sail. In 1885, for
the first time, there was more steam than sail
tonnage in the world's merchant fleets.

The screw propeller owed little to Scottish inventors and perhaps this is why the paddle steamer is still popular on Clydeside. The screw propeller developed rapidly in England and America in the 1830s and was adopted by the Royal Navy in the 1840s, being far better than paddles for warships. In 1850 Tod and McGregor launched the *City of Glasgow*, an early screw-powered Atlantic liner and two years later Denny built the *Andes*, Cunard's first iron screw ship.

Amid all this progress with steam, Scottish shipyards advanced the technology of sailing ships further than ever before. Free trade created demand for speed, as did the California and Australian Gold Rushes. The original clipper ship was an American development, but many of the most famous, such as the *Cutty Sark* and her rival *Thermopylae*, came from Scotland. Fast sailing ships were possible because the long peace after 1815 eliminated the need to carry guns, while the use of the steam tug to enter harbour allowed designers to concentrate more on deep-sea performance. Steel masts and wire rigging increased their sailing qualities, and crews were kept to a minimum (65).

New shipyards

From 1850, existing firms expanded, often moving down river to deeper water. Alexander Stephens went from Kelvinhaugh to Linthouse in 1870, across the river from a site used by Barclay Curle since 1852. Simons went from Whiteinch to Renfrew in 1860, while J and G Thomson travelled rather further, from Govan to Clydebank, in 1872. The ancient settlement of Govan was transformed, increasing its population tenfold between 1864 and 1904 (66). A new town was founded at Clydebank, named after the shipyard: it had grown to a population of 43,000 by 1913. In Dumbarton, Denny's moved across the River Leven to a new yard in 1869, then doubled its size by building on reclaimed land in the 1880s.

The shipbuilding business was subject to wild fluctuations, but over a period firms might expect to make unspectacular returns of 8–10 per cent on capital. Nevertheless, new companies moved into the industry from several directions. Firms which used ships, such as D & W Henderson of the Anchor Line, preferred to supply their own. Steel firms expanded to form 'vertically integrated' armament manufacturers, offering a full range of services in warship construction, including armour, guns and engines. Thus, in 1899, John Brown of Sheffield, threatened by rivals such as Vickers and Armstrong Whitworth, which already had shipyards as markets for their products, bought the J and G Thomson yard at Clydebank for £923,235, bringing one of the most famous names into Clyde shipbuilding. William Beardmore stayed closer to home. His business empire was based on Parkhead Forge in Glasgow. In 1900 he took over the former Napier yard at Govan and in 1905 he opened a vast new yard at Dalmuir, just downriver from Brown's. Intended to cater for the warship boom, it was called the Naval Construction Works, though in peacetime it was never as specialized as the title implied. It was built on a grand scale, with the first tower crane on Clydeside, a mould loft 300 ft (91 m) long, a shipbuilding gantry over the main building slip and vast engine and boiler shops.

A more truly dedicated warship yard was that set up by Alfred Yarrow in Scotstoun in 1906. The firm originated on the Thames and had specialized in destroyers and other small warships. Finding the waters too restricted and the wages too high, Yarrow fielded offers from every shipbuilding river in Britain before settling on the Clyde.

The layout of a shipyard

Office buildings often had a certain grandeur. At Fairfield they were in an Italianate style, with a sculptured figure of a workman on each side (colour plate 9). Denny's offices in Dumbarton (one of the few parts of the yard to survive) were more modest. On the ground floor they had a counting house, stationery

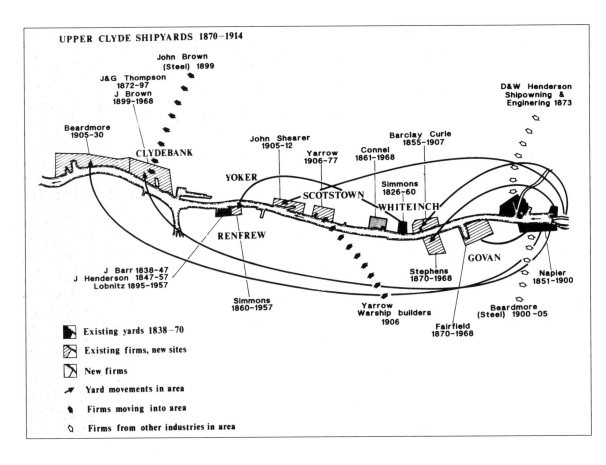

UPPER CLYDE SHIPYARDS 1870–1914

John Brown
(Steel) 1899

J&G Thompson
1872-97
J Brown
1899-1968

D&W Henderson
Shipowning &
Enginering 1873

Beardmore
1905-30

CLYDEBANK

John Shearer
1905-12

Yarrow
1906-77

Connel
1861-1968

Barclay Curle
1855-1907

YOKER

SCOTSTOWN

Simmons
1826-60

WHITEINCH

RENFREW

J Barr 1838-47
J Henderson 1847-57
Lobnitz 1895-1957

GOVAN

Napier
1851-1900

Simmons
1860-1957

Yarrow
Warship builders
1906

Stephens
1870-1968

Beardmore
(Steel) 1900-05

Fairfield
1870-1968

- Existing yards 1838–70
- Existing firms, new sites
- New firms
- Yard movements in area
- Firms moving into area
- Firms from other industries in area

66 Shipbuilders on the Upper Clyde, 1870–1914. Some firms moved down river, while new firms came into the industry from other parts of the country (Yarrow), from the steel industry (John Brown and Beardmore) and from other industries (D and W Henderson).

room, waiting room, luncheon room for 26 and individual offices for ten managers. Above was the drawing office with 30 benches. The 'Girls' Room' next door had ten benches for tracers; Denny's were among the first to employ women to copy drawings. Several hundred plans might be needed for each ship, including the lines plan which gave the shape of the hull, rigging plans, deck plans, cross-sections, constructional drawings of the frames and plating, fitting-out drawings for the cabins and saloons, scientific plans such as stability curves, and later, wiring diagrams.

In most yards the offices were next to the main gate, where every day at the end of working hours, hundreds of overall-clad workers streamed out, mounting bicycles or rushing for trains and trams. The workers' entrance often had separate doors for the various trades, reinforcing craft prejudices.

A few shipyards had their own test tank, in which models were pulled through the water to test their lines. The second in the world (after William Froude's at Torquay) was set up by Denny in Dumbarton in 1883 (67). John Brown set one up in 1904.

Ship models were also important in advertising the product. The 'builder's model' style had evolved by the 1880s. They were economically made, with a carved hull using the 'bread and butter' method of construction, with details such as doors and hatches painted or

67 The Denny Test Tank at Dumbarton. The facility is now operated by the Scottish Maritime Museum.

drawn on and standard items such as winches, ventilators and portholes mass-produced in metal. The main yards had their own model-making shops and there were several firms in Glasgow who made models for the smaller firms. The models were displayed in the yard offices, and shipped out to the great international exhibitions of the period.

Meanwhile, construction of the real ship began. From the drawing office, plans went to the mould loft where full-size patterns were made. The loft at Fairfield was 275 ft (83.8 m) long and 60 ft (18.3 m) wide and could be used simultaneously for the lines of four ships, each 600 ft (183 m) long (68).

Raw materials were delivered by rail and most yards had their own tracks and locomotives. Though railways ran down both sides of the Clyde by 1858, Govan was bypassed and Fairfield had to use part of the public tramway in Govan Road to transport iron and steel.

Plates and bars were stored in the open, to be weathered by rusting to remove mill scale.

The frames which formed the skeleton of each ship were made in the platers' shed by heating angle-iron until it was red hot and bending it against pegs in holes in the floor. The plates which would form the 'skin' of the ship were also bent indoors after the size, shape and curvature had been calculated from plans and models. All pieces were smoothed and drilled with holes before they went out to the building slips. These processes were increasingly mechanized over the years. Various types of ironworking machines were produced, for example, by Craig and Donald of Johnstone. They made punches which could cut holes as large as 30 in by 21 in, as well as drills, frame benders and plate bending machines (colour plate 7). Irregular shaped

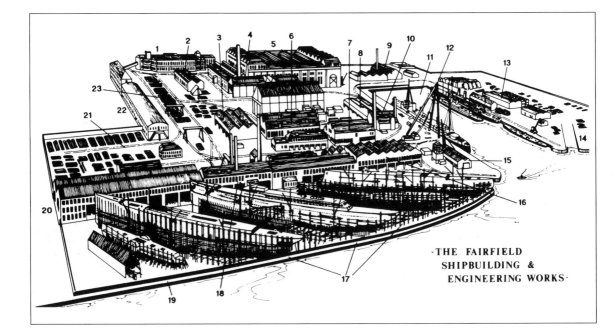

-THE FAIRFIELD
SHIPBUILDING &
ENGINEERING WORKS-

68 The Fairfield Yard as it was in 1909

1 Offices	13 Boat and Spar Shed
2 Pattern Shop	14 Timber Basin
3 Platers	15 Dock Workshop
4 Boiler Shop	16 Joiners' Shop
5 Engine Shop	17 Shipbuilding Berths
6 Plumbers	18 Ironworkers' Shed
7 Mechanics' Shop	19 Removable Timber Walkway
8 Sawmill	20 Smithy
9 Brass Foundry	21 Yard Railway
10 Power Station	22 Mould Loft
11 Fitting Out Basin	23 Steel Stockyard with Gantries
12 Sheer-legs	

pieces, such as the frame round the propeller which also formed part of the stern of the ship, had to be specially cast, often outside the shipyard. The machinery of the Clydebank shipyard was valued at £37,000 in 1884 and at £231,000 30 years later.

In most Clyde yards the building slips formed an acute angle with the bank, for it was impossible to launch ships at right angles into the narrow river. Fairfield had a river frontage of 2600 ft (792 m). At Clydebank, John Brown's took advantage of the entrance of the River Cart to launch the largest ships of their day. At Dumbarton, both Denny and McMillan launched into a bend in the River Leven. Despite the vagaries of the Scottish weather, no major Clyde yard covered its building slips, though this had been common in naval dockyards for some decades.

The structure of the ship was held together by metal rivets placed through pre-drilled holes and flattened by hammering. Steam machinery was introduced by McMillan of Dumbarton in the 1870s, with limited success. By the end of the century, hydraulic, pneumatic and electric riveting machines were common.

Launching

The launch of any ship, even the humblest cargo steamer, was a matter of some importance for the owner and builders, as well as the local community (69). The launch of No 534 at Clydebank in September 1934 went far beyond that, a national event for which The Times issued a special supplement in London. John Masefield, the Poet Laureate, was moved to verse:

'... a rampart of a ship'

69 The *Aquitania* ready for launch at Clydebank in 1914. The cranes on each side of the building berth were installed specially for the ship.

70 A crane on the Clydeside.

71 The Joiners' Shop in John Brown's in 1901.

Long as a street and lofty as a tower,
Ready to glide in thunder from the slip
And shear the sea with majesty of power.'

King George V, the Queen and Prince of Wales attended and it was Her Majesty who announced that the ship would be named after herself – *Queen Mary*. She broke a bottle of wine on the bows and the ship took 54 seconds to slide into the River, heard nationally in a pioneering BBC outside broadcast.

But a launch was not just a formal ceremony, like laying a foundation stone or cutting a tape. Before launch, the hull was set on a 'cradle', placed on slides, tallowed to allow the ship to move under the force of gravity. Great chains were used to restrain the ship once she

had entered the water. There was spectacle when the great hull slid down the ways, behind which was a real risk of disaster; in 1883 the *Daphne* capsized on launch at Linthouse with the loss of 124 lives and in 1916 the great battleship *Ramillies* ran aground at Beardmore's, causing thousands of pounds of damage.

Fitting out

After launch the ship would be towed to the fitting-out basin, to be equipped with engines, masts, cargo derricks, cabins and furniture. Most yards had a rectangular basin, open to the rise and fall of the tide. Some, such as Yarrow, fitted ships out alongside the river bank while Connel had no fitting-out facilities and relied on the hammerhead crane on Finnieston Quay nearby.

The tower crane has become the symbol of

72 The First Class Lounge of the *Aquitania* in 1914, with a reproduction of a tapestry showing a naval battle at the far end.

Clyde shipbuilding, but it appeared quite late in the day. Until after 1900, the dominant feature in most yards was the 'sheer-legs', an arrangement of three legs, one of which could be moved to vary the height and angle of the structure. One survived at Dumbarton until Denny's closed in 1963.

The earliest 'hammerhead' cranes were used at the fitting-out berths, to hoist in large items of machinery. The first was installed at Dalmuir in 1905, by the German firm of Benrather. Fairfield's great hammerhead crane was erected in 1912, replacing the old sheer-legs which were dismantled by the new crane and sold to Canada. Today the crane is a listed building, part of the Kvaerner yard.

Around its main building slip, Beardmore's built a large gantry to help in constructing the hull of the ship. From the 1900s a lighter type of cantilever crane began to appear round the building slips of the yards, on rails to move along the side of a ship. Barclay Curle's had 11 tower cranes from 1909. Many more were built by the engineering firm of Arrol, but their order book suggests that the Clyde yards were rather backward; by 1914 they had fitted them in Belfast, Tyneside and Barrow yards, but not on Clydeside (70). Beardmore's introduced the luffing-jib cranes to Clydeside in 1920 and these became common; by the 1930s the Clyde skyline was dominated by cranes.

Engine works were often attached to the shipyards. At Fairfield the works covered 20 acres (8 hectares). By 1909 it had facilities for manufacturing the latest steam turbines; cast-

ing the casings, boring them out, fitting the numerous blades for their rotors and bolting the whole assembly together. There were boiler-making shops, copper and brass foundries and tool rooms. At Stephens of Linthouse the engine works, erected in 1872, consisted of two machine halls side by side, equipped with overhead cranes. Denny's engine works was a separate facility nearly a mile up the River Leven and its products were transported by barge to the shipyard.

As well as shipwrights, platers, blacksmiths, angle-iron smiths, drillers, caulkers, riveters and helpers making the hull of the ships, hundreds of joiners, cabinetmakers and plumbers were needed for building passenger ships: but specific figures are rare, and varied according to the work in hand (71). The interiors of Atlantic liners became increasingly sophisticat-

73 Flats built in 1906 in Dumbarton Road, Dalmuir, with a pre-Dreadnought battleship carved on the wall.

ed in the second half of the nineteenth century, creating more highly skilled work for the finishing trades.

The largest and most elaborate of the Clyde's liners before World War I was the *Aquitania* of 49,000 tons, launched by John Brown's in 1914. She was fitted for 4202 passengers in three classes and a crew of 973. First-class accommodation included a Louis XVI style saloon inspired by French chateaux; a smoking room whose design was based on the Painted Hall at Greenwich, including copies of the paintings there; a dining room in Adam style, with panelled mahogany; and a garden lounge (72). Third-class passengers had to make do with a sparsely furnished dining room with long rows of chairs for 350 passengers and three-tier bunks in rooms segregated by sex.

Around the yards

Shipyard owners, in the Victorian philanthropic tradition, supported local charities and funded amenities. Thus Govan contains the Elder Library, Elder Park and two hospitals, as well as a working man's institute named after Sir William Pearce of Fairfield. Employers also built housing estates for their workers, though the motives for this were not purely philanthropic, in view of the need to lure men to the area.

The housing reflected and reinforced the class differences of the time, based on occupational status. The owners built large houses for themselves, often on the fringes of the town. The Denny family home at Helenslee, built in 1866–70, was 'a massive mansion climbing through three or four storeys to a French-roofed tower'. Some had country retreats in the Firth of Clyde, such as Robert Napier's mock-Jacobean mansion at Shandon. The managers were offered substantial dwellings. The General Manager of Beardmore's lived in Melbourne House in the hills above the yard, with a pillared entrance, marble stairway and a tennis court. Draughtsmen and foremen tended to live in cottages, often provided by the yards, or in superior tenements such as those built by Beardmore in Dumbarton Road, Dalmuir, with a carved relief of the battleship *Agamemnon* (73). Manual workers lived in slightly humbler flats. The Knoxland estate in Dumbarton was built between 1873 and 1890 by Denny in co-operation with the local building society. It includes three-storey tenements round a square, with terraced or semi-detached houses for foremen.

However, the class divisions among the manual workers were as strong as anything else. The unskilled workers had little hope of advancement as a regular apprenticeship was needed to become skilled. Among the artisans, the boilermakers and riveters who put the ship together saw themselves as superior in status and income. The finishing trades often looked outside shipbuilding for alternative employment, so their interests were different. All had their own unions, causing the 'demarcation' disputes which began as early as 1860, and which the popular press a century later saw as almost the sole cause of the industry's troubles.

On completion a ship went on its sea trials, still flying the flag of the shipyard rather than of the future owner. The Firth of Clyde was ideal for this and a measured mile for speed trials was laid out at Skelmorlie in 1866, on the suggestion of Robert Napier. It offered a depth of 33 fathoms (60 m), but in 1909 it was shown that an accurate test needed deep water and the old measured miles in England, such as Maplin Sands at the mouth of the Thames, were inadequate. The measured mile in Kilbrannan Sound off Arran, with a depth of 110 fathoms (201 m), is still in use.

Many other trades were affected by shipbuilding. The importance of the iron and steel industry is obvious enough. Firms like Weir Pumps attained international status, supplying pumping equipment for ships around the world. Professors Barr and Stroud of Glasgow University set up their famous optical business in the 1890s, largely to make range finders for the Navy. The Royal Navy began to exploit the services of the Clyde artisan when it set up its main torpedo factory at Greenock in 1908, moving it to Alexandria in 1937.

The pre-eminence of Clyde shipbuilding did not detract from the importance of dozens of shipyards in the rest of the country. In Aberdeen Hall-Russell, which originated with a firm set up in 1790, built some of the finest steel sailing ships and then specialized in fishing boats and small craft. In Dundee, the Caledon yard was set up by W. B. Thompson in 1874 and built yachts and tugs and Britain's first motor tanker, the Sebastian of 1913.

Continuing innovation

In 1879 Denny launched the *Rotamahama*, the

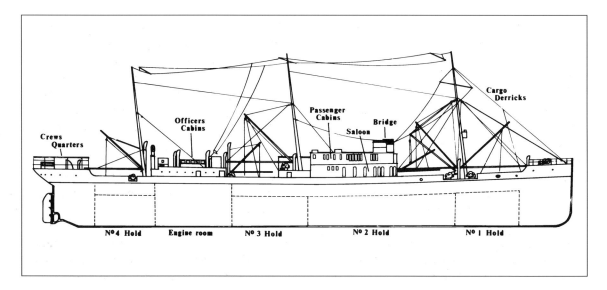

Saloon

Bridge

Nº 4 Hold   Engine room   Nº 3 Hold   Nº 2 Hold   Nº 1 Hold

74 *Jutlandia*, built by Barclay Curle in 1912.

first ocean-going ship of mild steel. Like the *Great Britain*, she proved the value of the new material by surviving grounding and it was found that 15 per cent of hull weight could be saved on steel ships. They became increasingly common over the next 20 years as the price of steel fell to equal that of iron. The *Strathleven*, launched at Port Glasgow in 1874, was the first purpose-built refrigerated ship. The *City of New York* and *City of Paris*, launched at Clydebank in 1888–9, were a major step in the evolution of the Atlantic liner, the first ships, apart from Brunel's failed *Great Eastern*, to exceed 10,000 tons and the first twin-screw ships on the route.

In the late nineteenth century Charles Parsons invented a new principle in steam power, an engine which employed a rotary rather than a reciprocating motion. Though his demonstration vessel, the *Turbinia*, was built on the Tyne, development soon moved to Scotland when Denny built the first turbine-powered merchant ship, the *King Edward*, in 1901, and followed it up with the *Queen*, the fastest steamer on the English Channel.

The diesel engine, invented by the German engineer of that name in 1892, was first used at sea in the *Selandia*, built in Denmark in 1911; but the Clyde was not far behind and the third ship, the *Jutlandia*, was launched by Barclay Curle in the following year (74). Clyde yards were involved in these developments which were to revolutionize ship propulsion, but they no longer had a commanding lead as in the 1870s and 1880s.

Shipbuilding for war

Between 1870 and 1914 the tonnage of ships launched on the Clyde oscillated with trade cycles, but in peak years the volume expanded regularly, so that 266,838 tons were launched in 1874, 516,977 tons in 1902 and 756,976 tons in 1913. In absolute terms, Clyde shipbuilding reached its peak in that year, or in 1908 when 569 ships were launched. Relatively the peak was in 1909, when the Clyde launched 39 per cent of British merchant tonnage, and 24 per cent of world tonnage.

Though Napier built some of the Royal Navy's first ironclads in the 1860s, warships played a small part in Clyde shipbuilding until 1889, when Parliament passed the Naval Defence Act, increasing the size of the Royal Navy so that it would be as large as the combined force of any two others and marking the beginning of an arms race that was to last until World War I. Since this was beyond the capacity of existing naval dockyards, the

Admiralty turned to private yards, including those on the Clyde.

The arms race accelerated after 1898 when the German Navy began to expand and in 1906 when HMS *Dreadnought* was completed in Portsmouth. With turbine engines and an all big-gun armament, she made existing battleships obsolete. Great public interest was shown, especially in 1909 when the popular slogan 'We want eight and we won't wait' symbolized a campaign which pressed the government into doubling the capital ship programme for that year. The process intensified as even bigger ships were produced. The first Dreadnought from the Clyde, the *Colossus* launched by Scotts of Greenock in 1911, was of 22,250 tons and had 12 inch guns. The 'super-Dreadnought' *Conqueror*, launched by Beardmore in the following year, was of 25,000 tons and had 13.5 inch guns. John Brown's *Barham* and Fairfield's *Valiant*, two of the most powerful battleships of the era, were of 33,000 tons with 15 inch guns. In all, the Clyde completed six battleships from 1911 to 1917, while Fairfield and John Brown specialized in fast, glamorous battlecruisers, building seven out of the Navy's twelve.

Smaller yards such as Denny, which never built a warship until 1907, began to take orders for destroyers and submarines. Yarrow, of course, specialized in this market and picked up orders for a dozen ships by 1914. Even so, warship production was never a large percentage of Clyde peacetime building. 1910 was a peak year, in which 19 warships were launched, of 42,534 tons, compared with 339 merchantmen of 349,858 tons.

With the outbreak of war in 1914, naval construction speeded up again. The main warship building yards, including Brown's, Beardmore's and Fairfield's, were taken under direct Admiralty control and almost ceased merchant ship building. Though few more battleships were begun, the Admiralty found itself short of smaller vessels for minesweeping and anti-submarine work. During the war 481 naval vessels were launched, with an average tonnage of 1578, and smaller yards which had never built warships were brought into the effort.

Beardmore's experimented with an aircraft carrier design as early as 1912. However, it was merely coincidence when the liner *Conte Rosso*, under construction in the yard, was converted to become the world's first true aircraft carrier, HMS *Argus*, launched in 1918. Thus in ten years a single yard had seen a whole generation of naval technology since building the *Agamemnon*, one of the last preDreadnoughts, in 1908.

The radicalism of Clydeside workers, combined with the government's attempts to 'dilute' the workforce with unskilled and female labour, led to a series of disturbances which later became part of the 'Red Clyde' legend. Though it was engineering workers who took most of the initiative, the trouble was sparked off in August 1915 when 430 Fairfield workers went on strike over the dismissal of two colleagues and 17 of them were jailed or fined.

The great depression

The years immediately after World War I were busy, as lost merchant tonnage was replaced. 1920 was a record year for British yards in which more than 2 million tons were launched, more than a third on Clydeside. After that there was a rapid decline as warship building came to a stop and few new merchantmen were needed.

There was a recovery in the late 1920s, but the second wave of the depression began in 1929. Three Clyde yards closed that year, two more in 1930, and three in 1934. In 1936 Harland and Wolff ended its Glasgow operation. McMillan's yard in Dumbarton was shut down by the National Shipbuilders Security Ltd, which was set up to reduce capacity in the industry, and the assets were sold in September 1932. The catalogue began with:

'Six 10-ton all-steel three-motor electric shipyard tower cranes
Two 5-ton steam loco cranes
2 all-steel electric derrick cranes'

75 The *Queen Mary* under construction at Clydebank.

It ended with the more mundane contents of the Counting House ('Set postal scales') and kitchen ('29 wine glasses, 10 tumblers, 2 decanters and 2 carafes'). The site became Dumbarton Distillery.

By 1932 more than 60 per cent of shipyard workers were unemployed, while the rate of unemployment for all workers was little more than 20 per cent. The Clyde launched only 49,000 tons of shipping in 1933, less than any year since 1870.

When it became known in 1930 that Cunard planned to build a gigantic new liner, the largest ship in the world, there was fierce competition but they were persuaded to place the order with John Brown's. Work began on the new ship, yard no. 534, the same afternoon as the contract was signed, but stopped two years later (75). It was not until April 1934, after Cunard had merged with the White Star Line, that building restarted. The town was decked with flags and pipers played as the workers returned. The ship, the *Queen Mary*, was launched in September 1934 and by that time the yard was almost ready to sign a contract on a slightly larger ship, later named the *Queen Elizabeth*.

The depression was a great blow to the self-confidence of Clyde shipbuilders, reinforced by the fact that control had passed to a new, less imaginative generation. The Clyde yards, the most innovative in the world before 1914, had become so fearful of change that in 1936 they sent a deputation to the Admiralty urging them not to adopt a system of longitudinal framing for a new class of destroyers, though a ship with such a system had been built by Denny in 1913.

The wartime revival

When relief came to the Clyde, it was in the ambivalent form of rearmament for another war. In 1937 orders were placed for five new battleships, the first since 1922, and Fairfield's and John Brown's got one each. By 1938 the Clyde had 165,000 tons of naval work in hand.

The 1939–45 war was fought intensely at sea, with many losses among ships great and small – none more dramatic than the blowing up of HMS *Hood*, a product of John Brown's, in 1941. The Clyde built comparatively few large warships and only two fleet aircraft carriers, *Implacable* and *Indefatigable*. However, Britain's last battleship, the *Vanguard*, was launched at Clydebank in 1944. Instead, the Clyde specialized in medium sized warships – cruisers and new types of anti-submarine escort, the sloops and frigates. But it was the destroyer at which the Clyde excelled and most of the famous Tribal Class, for example, were built there. The building of merchant ships was equally important to replace losses in the Battle of the Atlantic, and some of the yards built standard merchant ships: colliers and coasters by Ailsa of Troon, fast cargo liners by Caledon of Dundee. The old Harland and Wolff yard at Govan was reopened. The Clyde was further away from enemy airfields than any other shipbuilding area, but this did not prevent terrible raids on Clydebank on the nights of 13 and 14 March 1941, when more than 1000 people were killed and a third of the houses destroyed.

In the 12 years or so after 1945, Clyde shipbuilding enjoyed an Indian summer. The world merchant fleet had to be rebuilt after the horrors of the U-boat campaign, while the Cold War boosted warship orders. Germany and Japan were prostrate after wartime bombing while American shipbuilders were too expensive to break into the world market. This situation led to a certain amount of complacency, in which it was assumed that the world would always need 'Clyde-built' ships. Industrial relations became notoriously bad while yard managements, believing that the world boom would not last, failed to make adequate investments or preparations for the years which would follow.

The decline of shipbuilding

The years after 1956–7 saw great changes and the beginning of the end of Clyde shipbuilding as a world force. The size of oil tankers began to increase, reaching 200,000 tons in 1966 and nearly 500,000 tons by 1973; Clyde yards were too small to build such monsters. The former enemies, Germany and Japan, re-entered the industry and used the latest techniques. Denny had used welding in *Robert the Bruce* in 1934. It offered great advantages in strength, smoothness of hull and possibilities of prefabrication, but it was developed mainly by the Americans during World War II and adopted only slowly and cautiously on Clydeside. It was a similar story with prefabrication, in which much of the ship was built under cover. Although the notorious Scottish weather affected three days out of ten in the winter months, Clyde building berths remained unprotected from the rain until Yarrow's erected its first covered building slip in 1971. Meanwhile industrial relations worsened. Between 1965 and 1970, an average of 1.75 days were lost annually per employee, compared with 0.38 among other Scottish employees; 152,000 days were lost in 1970.

By 1962, the builders were aware of the need for modernization and in their advertising they described how yard layouts had been improved and welding adopted. Fairfield claimed, 'Old cranes at the berths have been replaced with new ones of 40 and 80 tons lifting capacity. ... Machines for cold-frame-bending, automatic butt and fillet welding of steel and aluminium, and automatic flame-cutting machines have been installed'.

1963 began with 60 empty berths and 6000 men unemployed. Two small yards closed and then, in July, Denny went into voluntary liquidation, partly because a £2m development programme had failed to bring in new work. In 1965 it seemed like a return to old times when the contract for a new ocean liner, later called the *Queen Elizabeth 2*, was awarded to the Clydebank yard. It turned sour as the yard made a loss, incurring penalty charges for late delivery. By 1965 there were three main yards on the lower Clyde at Greenock and six on the upper Clyde. Five of these, John Brown, Connel, Yarrow, Fairfield and Stephens, were merged in 1968 to form Upper Clyde Shipbuilders. In 1971 the government withdrew the subsidy and bankruptcy threatened. In the famous 'work-in', the employees mounted a massive public relations exercise which saved the firm for the time being.

In 1977 the shipbuilding industry was nationalized, despite strong opposition from the owners: Sir Alexander Murray Stephen had written of its 'deadening, soul-destroying hand'. In 1984-5 British Shipbuilders lost £238m and was privatized by the Thatcher government. Yarrow's came under the hammer: '58.6 acre South Street site in Scotstoun. These facilities include almost a mile of riverside together with administration and technical buildings. ... The company can build vessels of up to 200 metres in outside berths and vessels of up to 150 metres in covered facilities.'

It was bought by GEC and eventually became part of the Vickers Group. The old Fairfield Yard went to the Norwegian firm of Kvaerner and is the last yard in the United Kingdom building large merchant ships (colour plate 8). Ferguson make small ferries at Port Glasgow, and the Clydebank yard makes oil rigs, as does Scott Lithgow on occasion. The Clyde has reverted to its pre-1840 status as a minor player in world shipbuilding.

By the late twentieth century the yard sites had become restricted– it would never have been possible to build supertankers in such narrow waters – but many niche markets such as ferries, cruise ships and oil rig support vessels were missed. Today the Clyde's production is a long way behind yards in northern Italy, Germany and Denmark, not to mention the enormous facilities of Korea and Japan. Yet the shipyards shaped the urban geography of Govan, Clydebank, Dumbarton and Greenock.

6
Naval Scotland

On 6 August 1888 *The Glasgow Herald* carried the sensational headline, 'A Raid on the Clyde – Greenock Bombarded – The Town "in Ruins" – Booty Captured in Rothesay Bay'. A gunboat had entered the river, bombarded Greenock, forced the town of Rothesay to pay a subsidy and destroyed 32,000 tons of shipping in the lower Clyde. It went on to capture Oban.

In fact, it was a report on the Royal Navy's Annual Manoeuvres, in which the gunboat *Spider* had evaded blockading forces at Lough Swilly in Ireland and gone on to 'raid' Scotland. The gunfire heard at Greenock was blanks, but the local MP, Sir Henry Campbell-

Bannerman, complained that the Navy was 'causing needless disturbance and inconvenience to the inhabitants of the places visited, without any advantage to the naval service of the country'. The official report on the Manoeuvres was less passionate:

'While it may be considered extremely doubtful whether any cruiser ... could have done anything like the amount of damage claimed in the time, even if she met with no

76 The Martello tower at the entrance to Longhope Sound, Orkney, built in 1815 to protect the anchorage where Baltic convoys and whaling ships sheltered, and modified in 1866.

77 A fleet visit to Lamlash, Arran in 1901, drawn by F L
Blanchard from a sketch by Lieutenant E F Dugmore RN.

resistance, yet her movements show no great
obstacle lies in the way of an enemy's cruiser
entering any of the ports, including the Clyde,
which were visited by the *Spider* for a hostile
purpose, and this fact points to the necessity of
the proposed military defences of the latter
place being taken in hand as soon as possible.'

During the greater part of the nineteenth
century, Scotland was neglected by the Royal
Navy, which concentrated on plans for a war
against the traditional enemy, France, and on
operations in the British Empire. In 1853 a
report suggested that 'little is comparatively
known of the Royal Naval Service in Scotland,
from whence we believe that a much larger
number of excellent seamen might be obtained
than at present'. Early in the twentieth century
it was said that only 3 per cent of sailors came
from Scotland, because recruits were 'deterred
from joining by the great distance that separates
their homes from the existing naval ports'.
From the 1860s onwards Scotland only saw the
Navy when it made its annual cruise round the
British Isles and called at ports such as Lamlash
and Brodick in Arran, Scapa Flow, Cromarty
Firth and St Margaret's Hope in the Forth (77).
Such visits, which might last a fortnight in each

anchorage, were the subject of much celebra-
tion and often had a profound economic effect
on local communities such as Invergordon.

The Royal Naval Reserve, however, was
quite successful in Scotland. Formed in 1859, it
recruited professional seamen such as fishermen and ferrymen and drilled them in naval
practices, usually in old warships. Later the
Royal Naval Volunteer Reserve trained non-
seamen for the Navy. The most notable sur-
vivor of this is HMS *Unicorn* in Dundee, built
at Chatham in 1824 and the oldest British-built
warship afloat (colour plate 6).

The idea of a British naval base in Scotland
had first occurred two years after the Treaty of
Union and in 1709 Messrs Naish and Ward
were paid for a survey of the Firth of Forth.
But nothing was done and in 1895–1905 the
Royal Navy spent millions of pounds modern-
izing its bases at Chatham, Portsmouth and
Plymouth, but virtually nothing in Scotland. It
was only in 1903, as naval strategists began to
see the possibilities of war with the new
German Navy, that the Firth of Forth was
looked at again. The area had 'a valuable
strategic position in case of war with the northern powers'. Above the Forth Bridge at St
Margaret's Hope was to be found 'a large and
safe deep water anchorage already defended by
shore batteries, with an excellent approach at

all times. In close proximity to this anchorage is a convenient position on the north side where a basin, dockyard and other establishments could be placed, with ample room for expansion in the future along a shore fronting only agricultural land'. The decision to build a new naval dockyard at Rosyth was taken, but there were several years of delay because Admiral 'Jacky' Fisher, First Sea Lord from 1902 to 1910, regarded Rosyth as 'an unsafe anchorage' which would put 'the whole fleet in jeopardy', not to mention the risks from 'that beastly bridge which if blown up makes egress very risky'.

The building of Rosyth

Apart from Pembroke Dock, which never became a major base, the navy had not built an entirely new dockyard since Plymouth in 1690. The original idea was to build a base which would equal Chatham, Plymouth and Portsmouth in all respects, and handle the needs of a quarter of the Royal Navy. As well as a dockyard for ship repair, it would include a naval barracks, recruit training depot, ordnance depot, hospital, fuel storage, marine barracks and victualling base. This plan was gradually reduced to save money. In 1910 it was proposed that Rosyth should be developed gradually as a manning base for one-sixth of the fleet.

The dockyard itself was to be 'a small self-contained repairing base and in no way prejudicial to the larger scheme for a first class naval base'. The construction began in 1909, when the main contract was signed with Easton, Gibb and Son. The yard was designed round a large, square wet dock, created mainly by reclaiming land. Entry was by a lock on the east side of the basin, to be made by cutting through a large rock. There would be an emergency exit on the south side in case the main lock was blocked, but only one dry dock was planned, though more could be added later. There would be a submarine depot outside the wet dock, and electricity and pumping stations. A considerable amount of dredging would make a channel to the lock and the spoil would

be used to build up the banks to create space for new facilities. A 'garden city' would house the dockyard workers.

The design was subjected to serious criticism. By 1913 it was agreed that the planned depth of water in the basin needed to be increased from a minimum of 22 ft (6.7 m) to 36 ft (11 m), to allow the largest modern ships to use it. Because of the strong currents in the river, the emergency exit could only be used at slack water. A new exit was to be built on the east side, next to the main lock. It was also decided to have three dry docks instead of one. As a result of various delays, none of the facilities were ready when Britain entered World War I on 4 August 1914.

The Grand Fleet at Scapa

To operate in a war with Germany, Britain's Grand Fleet needed a base on the eastern side of the United Kingdom, where it could carry out a long range blockade of the German fleet in its main port at Wilhelmshaven, cover the coast against invasion and raids, and prevent the Germans from escaping into the Atlantic. It needed a sea area which was large enough not only to anchor the fleet, but to allow it to carry out training in gunnery and battle manoeuvres. It had to have relatively narrow entrances, so that it could be protected against attack by torpedo boat, and more especially the new threat of the submarine. The large anchorages on the east coast – Harwich, the Humber and the Forth – were either too open to be protected or too small to allow room for gunnery practice (78).

The great anchorage at Scapa Flow in Orkney had main entrances at Hoxa Sound in the south and Hoy Sound to the west, and several smaller ones which could be easily blocked by sinking old merchant ships. None was more than 2 miles wide. The base was close to the limit of the range of enemy submarines, though not beyond it, as some naval planners had assumed before the war.

Scapa Flow was surveyed by Graeme Spence of the Admiralty as early as 1812 and he concluded:

'In capacity it far exceeds any roadstead in Britain except Spithead, its area being upwards of 30 square miles and if it was all clean ground it would hold 60 sail of the line. ... Nature seems to have given every degree of shelter to Scapa Flow that could possibly be expected in a roadstead of such extent.' He did admit, however, that 'an objection will be made to it on account of the alleged danger of the navigation about Orkney from dangerous rocks and strong currents.'

It was used during many of the Fleet's annual cruises and before the war there was some interest in building a naval base, but it was almost completely unprepared when the Grand Fleet of 96 ships and 70,000 men arrived there on 29 July 1914, in anticipation of the declaration of war. Some of the more luxurious fittings of the ships, such as pianos and wardrobes, were landed on the beaches in anticipation of a quick battle and victory; but the fleet was to be based in the Flow for nearly four years and would fight only one major battle.

78 North Sea Naval Bases, 1914–18.

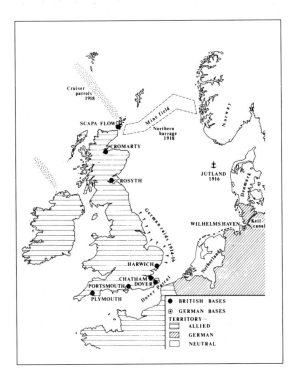

To the local population of 25,000, the arrival of a fleet which eventually outnumbered them four to one caused many social strains. Many served in the Territorial Army which had the duty of manning almost all the land defences in the early stages of the war. Others found much business serving the sailors and more especially the officers, as tailors and merchants, for example. They were soon subjected to strict controls on their movements, which caused much friction, while their basic puritanism was often offended by the exploits of drunken or high-spirited sailors.

The Navy, on the other hand, had to do much to make the Flow viable as a base (79). Men had to be fed and clothed, ships had to be repaired and refuelled, commanders had to be kept in constant communication with each other and with their superiors in London, while ordinary sailors needed to send letters home and have occasional leave. Since there was no time for extensive civil engineering work, most of the naval facilities were created afloat, in old warships or hired merchant ships. Depot and repair ships were anchored in the relatively protected waters of Longhope Sound and were equipped with all kinds of metal-working machinery. In 1917, a floating dock, capable of handling destroyers and smaller ships, was anchored in Gutter Sound, but cruisers and battleships still had to go to the dockyards in the south for major work. There were accommodation ships for dockyard workers, fishing craft were hired to service the warships, and cable links with the mainland were established. Preventing boredom among the sailors in ships which spent much of their time swinging at anchor, while their brothers in the army in France seemed to get all the glory, was perhaps the greatest problem of all. But one thing that was not available on board ship was space. The naval rating still loved his football, so from December 1914, the Marquis of Zetland gave the Navy the use of uncultivated lands on Flotta. Later golf courses were constructed and YMCA and Church Army huts were set up.

79 A boxing match on board the battleship *Queen Elizabeth* in Scapa Flow, *c.* 1917.

Even so, Scapa Flow was not a place where up to 100,000 seamen, mostly young and highly active, could find much contentment. Lieutenant Dawson wrote, 'for the first six months of the war we in *Dreadnought* never saw a tree, a train or a woman. Scapa Flow possessed no trees to all intents and purposes, no trains at all, and opportunities for going on shore were remote'.

Most ships at that stage were coal-burning, and the best steamship coal came from South Wales. More than 1500 colliers were to sail into the harbour during the war, bringing more than 4 million tons. Once alongside, the coal would have to be stowed aboard the ship by her own crew, a filthy, laborious task which was always done at the end of a gruelling patrol, so that the ships would be ready to go out again. In the course of the war most ships were converted to oil fuel, which saved much labour but had to be imported, mostly from the United States – 1.9 million tons were used in the war.

The biggest threat was from enemy submarines. As yet there was no way of detecting them underwater, unless a look-out was able to spot a periscope. This caused numerous false alarms, as in the first 'Battle of Scapa Flow' on 1 September 1914, when a light cruiser opened up at a supposed periscope. Several other ships fired and as darkness fell the fleet was ordered to put to sea. It took hours to get the warships and supply vessels underway, but later enquiry suggests that the whole thing was a false alarm. In view of this and other scares, the Flow was abandoned for a time and the fleet was decanted to west coast anchorages such as Loch Ewe, which were out of submarine range. Admiral Beatty describes the plight:

'The situation as it is, we have no place to lay our heads. We are at Loch na Keal, Isle of Mull. My picket boats are at the entrance, the nets are out and the men at the guns waiting for coal which has run low, but ready to move at a moment's notice. ... The men can stand it, but the machines can't, and we must have a place where we can stop for from four to five days every now and then to give the engineers a chance.'

80 Scapa Flow in 1916:

   a. Fleet anchorage.

   b. Fleet auxiliaries.

   c. Destroyer anchorage.

   d. Trawlers and drifters base.

   e. Hospital ships.

   f. Anchorage for ships exercising.

   g. Anchorage for merchant ships under examination.

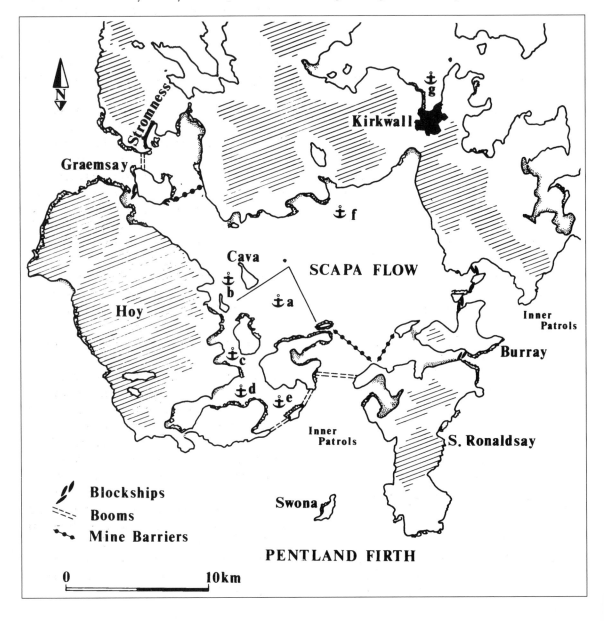

The only answer was to improve the anti-submarine defences at Scapa Flow. Blockships were sunk to stop up the minor entrances, underwater barriers were constructed and nets were laid across the main entrances, with 'gates' which could be opened and closed by fishing boats under naval command. The fleet was back by Christmas 1914, but improvements continued throughout the war. 'Observation' minefields, which could be made live electrically by an observer on shore, were installed across the main entrances during 1915, while conventional minefields were laid at other points (80).

On 30 May 1916 the Grand Fleet sailed out from Scapa on what most believed to be another routine patrol. The following day they were to encounter the German High Seas Fleet in the Battle of Jutland, the greatest sea battle ever fought in European waters, and the last fleet battle between surface ships, before the aircraft and the submarine established their dominance. Three British battle-cruisers blew up, but the German Fleet was driven from the area.

The Navy had its share of tragedy in the waters around Orkney. A few days after Jutland, the cruiser *Hampshire* left the Flow carrying Field Marshal Lord Kitchener on a special mission to Russia. She was sunk by a mine off Marwick Head and Kitchener was drowned. In July 1917 the 22,900 ton battle-ship *Vanguard* was at anchor north of the island of Flotta when she blew up, apparently accidentally. Only three men survived. The following month Commander Edwin Dunning made a great step in naval aviation in the Flow, when he landed his Sopwith Pup on the fore-deck of HMS *Furious* with the aid of men grabbing handles on the wings to stop the aeroplane. He tried again the following day and was lost over the side.

Anti-submarine warfare

As well as the threat to the Grand Fleet, the German U-boat threatened to cut off Britain's supplies after unrestricted submarine warfare was declared in February 1915. Imaginative and desperate attempts were made to find ways of detecting submarines and in 1916–17, in the public swimming baths and later in the open-air pool at Alexandria Park in Glasgow, sea-lions from a circus were trained to find submarines underwater; but they were completely unreliable and much preferred to chase fish.

Far more useful work was done in the Admiralty Experimental Station at Hawkcraig, near Aberdour in Fife. Under the leadership of Commander C P Ryan, scientists developed a system of fixed hydrophones which could detect submarines and, in combination with controlled minefields and anti-submarine patrols, could keep a fairly wide estuary free of danger.

On the other side of Scotland, Shandon Hydropathic Hotel was used by the Clyde Anti-submarine Committee. In the deep water of the Gareloch, they pioneered another approach (81). Instead of trying passively to detect the sounds submarines made, pinging noises were sent out on a transducer and the echo gave not only the bearing, but also the distance of an enemy boat. Further work at Parkestone Quay in eastern England completed the development of Asdic (later known as Sonar), which was to be the main anti-submarine technique of World War II, though it was too late to be used in this war.

The Northern Barrage was a very ambitious scheme to build a great minefield between Norway and Scotland to prevent German submarines from getting into the Atlantic. The barrage plan was backed by the Americans after their entry to the war in 1917, and only their spare industrial and shipping capacity made it possible. Mines were shipped from Virginia to the Clyde and then put on special trains to Inverness and Invergordon, where they were assembled and loaded into old American cruisers. More than 70,000 had been laid by the end of the war at a cost of $40m. After the war the US Navy cleared the barrage, operating from Scapa Flow with 5000 men.

81 (Top) Shandon Hydropathic Hotel on the east shore of the Gareloch, flying the white ensign as a naval establishment in 1918.

82 (Bottom) The dam used in the construction of the main entrance lock at Rosyth, May 1916.

The Navy in the Forth

Despite the difficulties, special measures were taken to open some kind of base at Rosyth on the outbreak of war in 1914. On 25 August the dam of the tidal basin was breached and it became available for small ships. Early in 1915 it was recognized that the war was going to be a long one and it was worth accelerating the completion of the yard. The main basin was available for naval use in March 1916.

From November 1914 the German High Seas Fleet raided English east coast towns. Though they did little strategic damage, there was pressure to move the Grand Fleet southwards, or to split it to cover the coast. Admiral Jellicoe, who had taken command on the outbreak of war, resisted strongly. Rosyth was 'admirably situated as a repairing base when the dockyard is completed, but it is not considered suitable for a war anchorage .... the anchorage below the Forth Bridge cannot be made secure against torpedo attack except at prohibitive cost'. A fleet based in the Forth would have no room to exercise free of the submarine threat, unless the wide entrance to the Firth was protected. However, the Battle Cruiser Fleet, the heavy scouting force and the most glamorous part of the Navy, was based in the Forth from early 1915. There were few

83 The battleships *Canada*, *Collingwood* and *Warspite* in Rosyth Dockyard, September 1916.

opportunities for it to practise gunnery, and this had a serious effect on its performance in battle.

On 1 June 1916 some of the casualties of Jutland arrived at Rosyth. The great battleship *Warspite* was docked right away, followed next day by the battlecruisers *Princess Royal* and *Tiger*, and then Beatty's flagship the *Lion* (82, 83). The dockyard was formally handed over to the Navy in November 1917.

By 1918 the facilities of the Forth area had been greatly improved (84). They included a destroyer base at Port Edgar on the south side of the river, a hospital at Granton, an ordnance depot at Crombie, and a victualling establishment in Grangemouth. A new anti-submarine defence line had been set up between Elie in Fife and the island of Fidra near North Berwick, creating a safe area even bigger than Scapa Flow, in which the Navy could anchor and exercise. In April 1918 the Grand Fleet steamed out of Scapa Flow and anchored in the Forth, where it was closer to supplies of all kinds, though oil was something of a problem. A pipeline was constructed following the line of the Forth and Clyde Canal from Bowling to

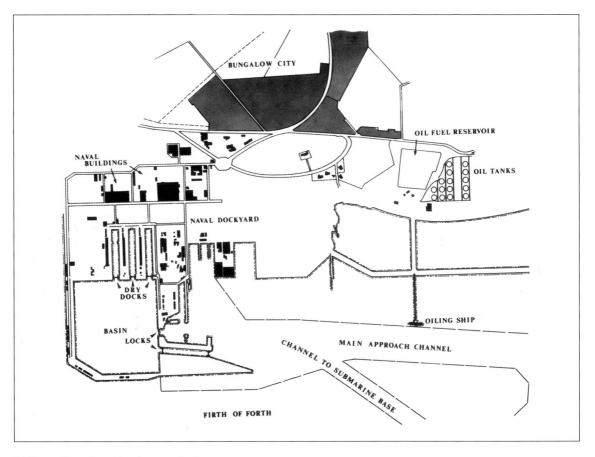

84 The naval complex at Rosyth, as completed.

Grangemouth, supervised by American engineers who had experience of such things, but it was not in service until two days before the war ended.

The High Seas Fleet at Scapa

At the end of 1918 another fleet entered the Forth in very different circumstances. Under the terms of the Armistice which ended the war on 11 November, the German High Seas Fleet was obliged to surrender 74 ships, including its ten best battleships and all six battlecruisers. Ten days later they steamed into the Forth and Admiral Beatty addressed his men:

'They are now going to be taken away, and placed under the guardianship of the Grand Fleet at Scapa, there they will enjoy (laughter) as we have enjoyed, the pleasures of Scapa. (laughter).'

Then he made the signal which ended the naval war:

'The German flag will be hauled down at sunset today, Thursday, and will not be hoisted again without permission.'

At Scapa the German fleet was anchored in a great semi-circle round the small island of Cava. The skeleton crews became increasingly demoralized, particularly after 11 May 1919 when they learned of the savage terms of the Treaty of Versailles. Among many humiliations, the interned ships were to be handed over and Germany was to be allowed a tiny fleet with a maximum of six battleships and no submarines. Admiral von Reuter, in command of the ships at Scapa, had already made plans and on Midsummer Day 1919, when the British fleet was out on exercises, his men opened the sea-cocks and allowed the ships to sink (85). A party of

85 German destroyers sinking off the island of Fara in 1919.

local schoolchildren, on a day trip round the harbour, watched in amazement. One of the adults described the scene:

'Some went down with their sterns almost vertical above the water, others listed to port or starboard with vast clouds of steam and rivers of oil pouring out of their vents and bubbling to the surface after the ships had reached the bottom and there was the roaring of escaping steam and the shouts of thousands of sailors as they made off in the boats.'

Twenty-two of the German ships failed to scuttle themselves, or were rescued and beached by British forces; but the pride of the German Navy had sunk to the bottom.

Perhaps it was not such a disaster for the former allies, who were already beginning to quarrel over who should have the surrendered ships. Arrangements were soon made to salvage them, as scrap iron rather than as fighting ships. In 1924 the firm of Cox and Danks bought 28 of them. They were raised one by one and towed south to the Forth, to be broken up in the former naval dockyard at Rosyth. The largest, the 28,000 ton battle-cruiser *Hindenburg*, proved the greatest challenge. In 1930 she was finally raised at the third attempt. The last ship, the *Derfflinger*, sister to the *Hindenburg*, was not raised until 1939 and finally broken up at Faslane in 1946. Eleven ships, including three battleships, remain on the bottom of the Flow.

The Invergordon Mutiny

With the end of World War I, the Navy largely withdrew from Scotland. The depot ships at Scapa Flow sailed away and land owned by the Admiralty was mostly sold off. The brand new dockyard at Rosyth was put on a care and maintenance base in 1923 and the Royal Navy returned thankfully to its bases in the south of England.

Cruises and manoeuvres still brought the Fleet to Scotland occasionally, so in September 1931 17 ships, including seven battleships and five cruisers, were anchored in Cromarty Firth, off Invergordon, as part of the autumn exercises of the Atlantic Fleet. This area had been developed by the Navy before and during World War I, and Admiral Fisher had preferred it to Rosyth as a minor base.

On Sunday 13 September 1931, Rear-Admiral Wilfred Tompkinson was forced to announce that, due to the international financial crisis, the pay of all ranks was to be cut by a shilling (5p) a day. A Lieutenant-Commander would lose only 3.7 per cent, while an Able Seaman, on 4 shillings a day, would lose 25 per cent of his wages, already meagre for a married man. There were deeper causes of discontent, for the class, promotion and social system of the Navy had failed to keep up with developments in society at large. As a result, on Monday 14 September, the seamen from several ships gathered in the shore canteen north of Invergordon and the talk turned to action:

'We decided to – well, more or less down tools, go on strike, that's what we called it. ... then we heard a banging at the door. Someone looked out of the window and said, "It's the Officer of the Patrol". We'd got the door on a latch so that he couldn't push in if he wanted to.'

Lieutenant Robert Elkins was admitted and addressed the men, but one hothead threw a glass at him – the only act of violence in the whole affair. More speeches were made in the playing fields around the town, then the men went back to their ships.

Next morning, the men refused to turn out of their hammocks and the battleship *Repulse* was booed when she sailed out. Cheering spread from ship to ship and the men on the battleships refused to weigh anchor. Officers reacted in different ways, but all were aware that they had lost their authority. In London, the Admiralty and the government had to decide whether to crush the action by force or to conciliate the men.

The British Navy was still regarded as the greatest fleet in the world and news of the 'mutiny' caused the name of the small Scottish port to be flashed round the world. British shares fell and the government was forced to abandon the Gold Standard. The ships at Invergordon were ordered to sail for their home ports and the seamen, feeling that they had made their point, agreed to this. No-one was ever charged with mutiny relating to the affair, but 24 men were dismissed from the service. The effect of the pay cut was mitigated and no man was to suffer a reduction of more than 10 per cent.

U47 and the Churchill Barriers

When the threat of war with Nazi Germany became too obvious to ignore, Rosyth was re-opened as a dockyard and the Admiralty began to turn to Scapa Flow again, hoping to be better prepared than last time. Since the fleet was now fuelled by oil, storage tanks for 100,000 tons were built at Lyness, on the island of Hoy, in 1937. Shore accommodation was to be provided for 650 sailors and civilians.

On the 14 October 1939, six weeks after World War II began, the Royal Navy suffered another trauma. The German submarine *U-47*, commanded by Gunther Prien, succeeded in getting between sunken blockships in Holm Sound. Fortunately, the main Fleet had left the day before, but Prien managed to fire five torpedoes into the battleship *Royal Oak*, a veteran of Jutland. Just after one o' clock in the morning her crew were wakened by the explosions and began a scramble to safety as the ship slowly capsized. Eight hundred and thirty-three officers and men were lost out of 1400.

As a result, it was decided to block off the eastern entrances to the Flow through Holm and Water Sounds, though the 'Churchill Barriers' were not begun until August 1941 (colour plate 10). The water was nearly 60 ft (18.3 m) deep in places, currents could run up to 12 knots and some of the sounds were more than a mile wide. During the busiest time in 1943, 1720 men were employed, including 1,200 Italian prisoners of war. One of them, an artist, Domenico Chiocchetti of Trento, created a beautifully decorated Roman Catholic Chapel in Lamb Holm (colour plate 12). However, like the Barriers themselves, the Chapel was only completed after the need had passed. The Barriers (which were renamed causeways to make it legal to employ prisoners of war on them) were officially opened four days after the German surrender in 1945, while the Chapel had its first sung mass in 1959.

Scapa Flow remained as unpopular with the seamen as it had been 25 years earlier. Ludovic Kennedy, then a junior officer on a destroyer, wrote:

'The islands were treeless, just heather and grass, seabirds and sheep, and across the bare face of the Flow tempests blew, often for days on end. There were no women, shops, restaurants, just a couple of canteens that dispensed warm beer, a hall for film shows and the occasional concert party, and fields that too often displayed the sign "All grounds unfit for play".'

Scapa remained important as a base for operations against the German invasion of Norway and for supporting the Arctic Convoys to Russia. Ships set out to sink the *Bismark* in 1941 and the *Scharnhorst* in 1943, but the Flow was never the centre of the naval activity as it had been for most of World War I. The Germans had no battle-fleet as such, so there was no need for a great fleet anchorage. Instead, much of the sea war was about convoys and amphibious landings. In these, it was the bases in the Firth of Clyde which played a leading role.

The Clyde convoy base

As World War II approached, the Germans rebuilt their U-boat fleet. The Royal Navy had a good deal of faith in Asdic, but it was also aware that the bombing could close the southern and eastern English ports, such as London and Hull, which accounted for more than 40 per cent of British trade in the 1930s. The problem was greatly exacerbated with the Fall of France in 1940. The

Germans could operate the U-boats from French bases, ports such as Bristol were within easy bombing range, and the English Channel was hazardous. Supplies had to be brought into the country round the north of Ireland, using the ports of Londonderry, the Mersey and the Clyde.

Before the war the Clyde ports had been relatively small compared with London and Liverpool, accounting for less than 4 per cent of British trade. Glasgow had dealt mainly with liner traffic, with cargoes of 2000 to 5000 tons, whereas in wartime it had to handle ships carrying 10,000 tons each. It had mainly handled exports, whereas imports were now the priority. There were only 3600 dockers in Glasgow, but 5–6000 would be needed. The road and rail links at Glasgow Docks were adequate for the pre-war local trade, but not for the new demands.

Naval ships used the anchorage at the Tail of the Bank, off Greenock, though it was dangerous in gales. A boom was set up between Cloch Point and Dunoon to keep out U-boats, and 50 anchor berths for merchant ships were laid out off Kilcreggan, with 40 more in Loch Long, 5 in the Holy Loch and 26 in the Gareloch (86).

Two imaginative schemes were implemented. One was the 'overside discharge' of cargoes from newly arrived ocean-going ships into small coasters, which would then unload at the smaller Clyde ports or carry the cargoes onward. Dockers were sent up from London, which was underemployed in the circumstances, and coasters were collected from around the country. Overside discharge began in September 1940, but in practice it accounted for only about 3 per cent of goods on the Clyde. However, it was useful when the river was crowded with shipping.

The other scheme was the building of two entirely new ports in western Scotland – No 1 Military Port at Faslane on the Gareloch, and No 2 at Loch Ryan near

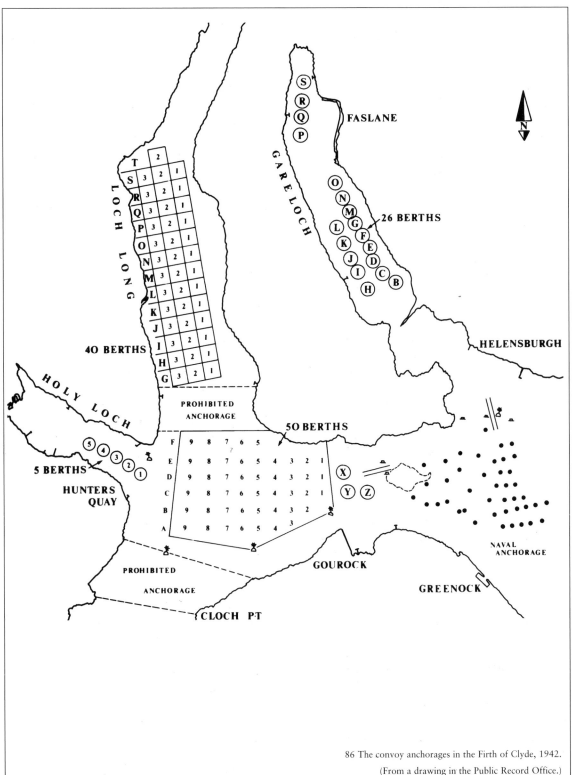

86 The convoy anchorages in the Firth of Clyde, 1942.

(From a drawing in the Public Record Office.)

Stranraer. With the withdrawal from France in June 1940 it was decided to set up two ports exclusively for exporting troops, military vehicles and supplies to combat areas around the world. The Gareloch was largely undeveloped before World War II, apart from hotels such as Shandon Hydro and as an anchorage for shipping laid up in the depression. Thus Para Handy's friend Hurricane Jack found himself 'An Ideal Job' as shipkeeper of 'a great big whupper o' a barquenteen caaled the *Jean and Mary*, wi' a cabin the size o' a Wee Free Church'.

The Faslane site was chosen because 'it gave the depth of water required, had the prospects of good ground to construct upon, and was within easy access of the West Highland Line of the London & North Eastern Railway'. The sea bottom was difficult to work with and special techniques had to be developed to sink piles in order to build jetties. The entrance to the Loch at Rhu Point had to be dredged to make it accessible to large troopships. The banks had to be built up to make room for railway sidings and parks for military equipment (87). The port began operating in the middle of 1941 and was complete by the end of 1942. It was the main centre for the heavy equipment used in the North African Landings in 1943.

As a result of the various efforts, the Clyde was able to handle about 20 per cent of British shipping needs during key periods of the war.

'The Terror of Tobermory'

By 1940 the west coast of Scotland was safer than other parts of the United Kingdom from bombing and submarine attack, not to mention the threat of invasion. There were many isolated and under-used harbours with good access to deep water or to beaches where invasion techniques could be practised, where seamen could be kept away from many of the distractions of shore life and work could be carried out in relative secrecy. Basic and

technical training were still carried out in the traditional naval bases, but many specialist activities were developed in Scotland, especially in the new fields of naval aviation, submarines and amphibious warfare.

Many small town hotels were taken over as messes, offices and training bases and gained exotic names – thus the Port Bannatyne Hydropathic, near Rothesay, became HMS *Varbel* and the Keil Hotel in Campbeltown was the Royal Naval Hospital. Largs became the centre of training for amphibious warfare. It was there in June 1943 in the former Hollywood Hotel, known as HMS *Warren*, that Lord Louis Mountbatten persuaded the Chiefs of Staff that the invasion of Europe should take place on the beaches of Normandy. The main anti-submarine training base was at Campbeltown, and also a headquarters for rescue tugs for ships damaged in the Atlantic.

But the most famous, or notorious, of Scottish training bases was HMS *Western Isles*, in Tobermory Bay, used for the working-up of destroyers and escort vessels. The commander, Commodore Sir Gilbert 'Monkey' or 'Puggy' Stephenson became one of the legends of the war. The Navy expanded nearly sixfold in the first five years of conflict; in peacetime officers had undergone more than six years of training before being commissioned, but now they could become sub-lieutenants in the Royal Naval Volunteer Reserve after three months on the lower deck followed by a three-month training course. Men put to sea after a few months in shore training schools. Hundreds of new escort vessels were commissioned to fight the U-boats in the Battle of the Atlantic and often reached Tobermory with only a few key men who had been to sea before. Stephenson's job was to 'work up' the ships, making them ready for action after 14 days of intensive and unconventional training.

His headquarters were in the converted passenger ferry HMS *Western Isles*, anchored in

Aros Bay at the eastern end of Tobermory Harbour. Much of the training was done in the waters nearby, with friendly submarines acting as mock targets. But the most important resource was the energy, determination and imagination of Stephenson himself, who spared no efforts to make the officers and men aware what they would have to face in the Atlantic. Kenneth Baker, the former newsreader who served in the Navy during the war, provides what he calls the 'authorised version' of a celebrated incident. The Commodore came on board a corvette one winter's morning:

'Without any preliminaries he flung his gold-braided cap on the deck and said abruptly to the Quartermaster – "That is a small unexploded bomb dropped by an enemy plane. What are you going to do about it?" The sailor, who had evidently heard about these unconventional tests of initiative, promptly took a step forward and kicked the cap into the sea. Everyone waited for a great roar of protest from the Commodore. But not at all. He warmly commended the lad on his presence of mind, and then, pointing to the submerged cap said: "That's a man overboard! Jump in and save him!"'

Stephenson earned his nickname 'the Terror of Tobermory', but 1132 ships were trained under his command.

Submarine bases in Scotland

When war broke out in 1939, the main Scottish base for submarines was at Dundee, where ten boats were stationed. The depot ship *Cyclops* arrived in Rothesay Bay in June 1940. Potential submarine commanders set out from her on practical courses, the forerunners of the notorious 'Perishers' course of post-war years, so-called because failure would bar the candidate from any further appointments in the submarine service. Edward Young, the first reserve officer to command a submarine, describes his experiences in 1943:

'I swept [the periscope] rapidly across the green shores of Bute, ... swung past the entrances to Loch Fyne and Kilbrannan Sound,

and continued along the steep shores of Arran, which rose nearly three thousand feet to the imposing summit of Goat Fell. The only ship in sight apart from the target was an outward-bound merchantman steaming down the main channel of the Firth of Clyde. Completing the circle I came back once more to the target, still going away to the eastward. ... Waiting for the *White Bear* to turn, I felt horribly uncertain of myself. ... In as calm a voice as I could muster, I gave the order, "attack team close up."'

The Rothesay area provided the facilities for training the crews of chariots or 'human torpedoes' and the famous x-craft, or midget submarines. Loch Striven, north of Rothesay, was sufficiently fjord-like and inhospitable to test the men for attacks in Norwegian waters. The operational base for chariots and x-craft in home waters was HMS *Bonadventure*, a submarine depot ship moored in Loch Cairnbawn in the extreme north-west of the Scottish mainland. From there in September 1943 six conventional submarines towed out a similar number of x-craft to attack Germany's greatest battleship, the *Tirpitz*, and other ships in Norwegian fjords. They immobilized her, though it took a bombing raid in 1944 to sink her.

In the Holy Loch for most of the war the depot ship was the *Forth*, headquarters of the Third Submarine Flotilla which in May 1944 consisted of 21 British boats of the S, T and U classes as well as three submarines manned by the Royal Netherlands Navy and two by the French. The flotilla attacked enemy shipping in the North Sea and the approaches to the Baltic. Six boats failed to return during the war and are commemorated on the war memorial at Lazaretto Point on the shores of the Loch.

The Clyde bases were still important after the war. In 1953–4 the Admiralty regarded a submarine war in the Atlantic as a serious threat and the anchorages in the Holy Loch and Gareloch were reserved for convoy operation. The former was ruled out as a submarine base because it would 'already be overcrowded with moorings laid by Port Emergency Planning staff'. Rothesay was to be the main

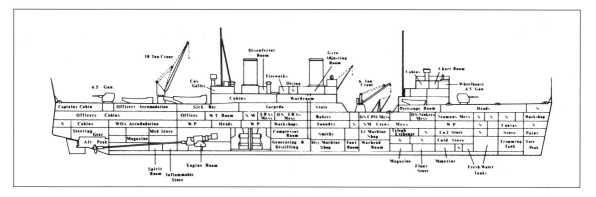

87 The submarine depot ship HMS *Forth*. Built by John Brown in 1939, she served in the Holy Loch 1940–1 and 1942–7, as head-quarters of the 2nd and 3rd Submarine Flotillas.

centre for UK-based submarines on the out-break of war, with three flotillas based there. It was suggested that an old battleship, *King George V*, which was then laid up in the Gareloch, might be converted to serve as a depot ship.

After 1956, all this was to change. The development of the hydrogen bomb and the intercontinental ballistic missile made it easy to wipe out the ports, so a new Battle of the Atlantic was unlikely. The battleship was irrele-vant, so older bases like Scapa Flow and Invergordon could be closed. The Holy Loch and Gareloch were now available for other uses. The Americans already had their eye on the former, while in 1960 the Gareloch was to see the end of the old navy when the last bat-tleship, the *Vanguard* of 1946, was towed there to be scrapped.

The US Navy in the Holy Loch

The missile-carrying nuclear submarine, known as the SSBN in the jargon of the US and later the Royal Navy, is still perhaps the most devas-tating weapons system yet devised by man. It can hide underwater for months at a time and can launch several missiles (usually 16) which are almost unstoppable and each of which con-tains more destructive power than all the bombs dropped in World War II. The United States Navy fired its first Polaris missile from a

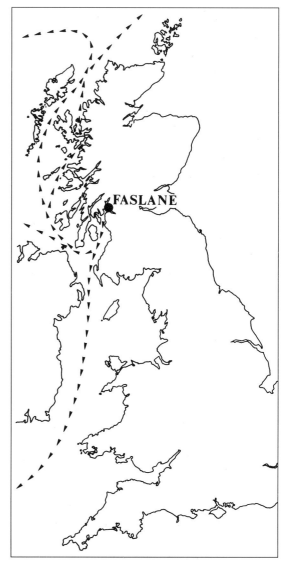

88 Submarine exits from the Firth of Clyde.

89 The US Depot ship *Canopus* in the Holy Loch with submarines, 1972.

submerged submarine in 1958.

The range of the submarines is practically unlimited, but the range of the Polaris missile itself was only 2500 miles, so the boats had to patrol some distance from the United States to act as a deterrent against the Soviet Union. Crews need to come ashore some time, so the Americans needed a base in European waters as a complement to their eastern one in Guam. In November 1960 the British government announced that an American depot ship would be stationed in the Holy Loch. The reasons for the choice are still shrouded in secrecy and retired naval officers questioned it, suggesting that it was too far from the sea and that the mouth of the Clyde could easily be blocked by mines as soon as a war started. But this perhaps misses the point about the new type of submarine. Its most important work was deterrence and it could be said to have failed if war began on that scale. To

be successful, the submarines had to be able to evade enemy shadows in peacetime, and the topography of the Clyde was helpful here. There were many different exits, along the north or south of Ireland, through the Minches or the Kyles of Lochalsh, for example. Each of these involved passing through territorial waters, from which rivals could be excluded in peacetime (88).

USS *Proteus* arrived in the Loch in 1961 and was met with sustained demonstrations from supporters of the Campaign for Nuclear Disarmament. However, the base had a profound effect on the local economy, making Dunoon the town with the highest proportion of taxi drivers in Europe. The base closed in 1992.

HMS *Neptune*

After the failure of the British Blue Streak and the American Skybolt air-launched missile projects, the British government signed the Nassau Agreement with the United States in December 1962, allowing them use of Polaris missiles. In March 1963 it was announced that the main

operating base for British Polaris submarines would be at Faslane in the Gareloch, already used for conventional submarines. This site was preferred to the alternative, Plymouth, because 'the use of Devonport as an operating base for nuclear submarines would be tantamount to siting a land-based reactor in a populated area'. But Faslane was still accessible by road, rail and river from Glasgow and other major centres of population. Like the American base in the Holy Loch, it had easy access to

90 The Faslane base in 1997, showing the new construction to the north of the old one. The most prominent building contains the shiplift, with a finger jetty just south of it, equipped with a crane.

deep water through a variety of exit routes.

The decision caused protest in Scotland on several levels. There was a strong campaign by CND, while the growing Scottish Nationalist movement suggested that such a base would not be sited so close to an English city. Metal

Industries, which leased part of the site as a shipbreaking yard, was unwilling to give up its tenure and stated, 'The great advantages of Faslane as a shipbreaking yard are the depth of approach, the depth alongside at low water and the length of the quays'.

The new base was not to rely on a depot ship, though a floating dock was installed for repairs. Stores, barracks, messes and training and engineering facilities were built on shore and the main road, which had run through the centre of the site, was realigned. Bunkers were built in Glen Douglas and an armament depot at Coulport in Loch Long. The new base, HMS *Neptune*, was opened in August 1967 and the first British Polaris submarine, *Resolution*, was commissioned two months later.

In the late 1970s the British government decided to adopt the Trident nuclear missile system, which required much bigger submarines and HMS *Neptune* was expanded at a cost of £1.7bn. The new base, which included a shiplift capable of raising a 5000-tonne submarine, was formally opened in August 1993 (90). The first Trident submarine, a new HMS *Vanguard*, arrived there in July 1992 and the last Polaris boat, the *Repulse*, sailed to Rosyth for decommissioning in August 1996.

From 1987 the Royal Dockyard at Rosyth was operated by Babcock Thorne and it was sold to them at a price of £20.5m in 1996. The Navy ceased to use it as an operating base in 1995, transferring nuclear submarine refit work to Devonport. Rosyth is still used by the Navy for storing and decommissioning nuclear submarines, while Babcock Thorne's work includes refitting of naval vessels.

During the Cold War, Scotland's northerly position was vital in patrolling and servicing the GIUK (Greenland, Iceland, United Kingdom) Gap. In an attempt to monitor Soviet submarines entering the Atlantic, lines of underwater surveillance buoys and controlled mines were laid in the sea and patrolled by surface ships, submarines and aircraft. It is three times as long as the Northern Barrage of 1918.

Scotland and the Royal Navy

No sea battle has been fought in Scottish waters since medieval times, but Scotland, though some distance from the main areas of naval conflict, has had a major role in providing support for the British and NATO navies. It is the furthest part of the UK from traditional enemies such as France and Germany, therefore safer for training and port operations in the age of submarines and bombers. It offers some control over the northern exit from the North Sea and Arctic Ocean into the Atlantic. The complex navigation of the west coast provides good training areas and many places for submarines to hide. Bases in Scotland are traditionally close to industrial skills and facilities in the central belt, though it is questionable whether these survive today in sufficient strength.

Scotland has never claimed to 'rule the waves' like England or the United Kingdom. Despite this, the British Navy at different stages in its history has relied heavily on Scottish officers and seamen, Scottish-built ships and Scottish bases. Maritime history has played a great and largely unrecognized part in developing Scotland and the sea remains important to this day, despite the decline of traditional shipping and shipbuilding. Two maritime themes – the oil industry and the presence of nuclear submarine bases – are still at the forefront of Scottish politics.

Places to Visit

Sites

Apart from documents and pictures, maritime history can be studied with the aid of different kinds of artefacts, buildings and geographical sites. The most obvious are the ships themselves. Some of these are archaeological items, dealt with in a companion volume by Colin Martin. Buildings are also to be included in the study of maritime history – shipyard workshops and offices, docks, breakwaters, cranes and lighthouses. Finally, the sea itself, and its interface with the land, is the most basic source of all. Conditions off the **Mull of Kintyre** or in the **Pentland Firth** can tell us much about the development of different areas of Scotland. The maritime historian is fortunate in that conditions at sea changed less than on shore – no-one builds towns or motorways there and tides and currents are practically the same as they always were. But even this needs some qualification, especially near the great cities. The Clyde is a very different river now from the one it was in 1760.

Early boats

Scottish logboats, mostly found locally, are on display in the many museums; a pillar at **Bantry** in Ireland provides the only contemporary physical evidence of the Celtic curragh. Virtually all the visual evidence on the West Highland galley comes from tombstones, especially at **Rodel, Harris, Iona Abbey** and less accessibly in **Colonsay Priory**.

Harbours

Most of the best natural harbours, such as **Scapa Flow** and **Cromarty Firth**, were taken over by either the Royal Navy or the oil industry during the course of the twentieth century, though in general they are large enough to cope with this intrusion and still show much of their original state. There are hundreds of small and attractive harbours round the coast and most are accessible. Personal favourites include **Crail, Portsoy, Tobermory** and **Pittenweem**, representing different styles and functions. Nothing can be seen of the dykes used in the original deepening of the River Clyde, but the **Lang Dyke** at **Dumbuck** can be seen best from Dumbarton Castle at low tide.

Clyde steamer piers

The **Dunoon** area contains an excellent collection of piers, showing many stages of development. David Napier's original at **Kilmun** has been extended by timber piling. **Dunoon Pier** itself is now the grandest on the Clyde, since Gourock has become dilapidated and Rothesay, damaged by fire in 1962, gives more prominence to its Victorian toilet. Dunoon Pier was built in approximately its present form in 1897-8 and the buildings on it were reconstructed in 1937. **Ardnadam Pier** was in naval use from 1940 to 1992. A yacht marina is being developed nearby. **Hunter's Quay** has a ramp for car ferries. **Kirn** and **Inellan** are in poor condition but still show something of their former use.

Nineteenth-century docks

Until recently **Leith Docks** were largely inaccessible to the public, but the display of the former Royal Yacht *Britannia* is beginning to change that. At **Dundee**, see the **Victoria Dock** of 1833 and the **Camperdown Docks** of 1857. At **Greenock** the **East India Harbour**, built by John Rennie in 1805-9, is visible from the main road. **Peterhead** has a complex arrangement of harbours and breakwaters, much used by fishing boats and the oil industry. The best known of the **Glasgow** docks, the **Queen's Dock**, has been filled in, as has most of the **Princes Dock** across the river in **Govan**. Survivors include **Rothesay Dock** in **Clydebank** and the **King George V Dock** at **Sheildhall**. The graving docks at **Govan**, built between 1869 and 1898, can be viewed from Govan Road. **Yorkhill Quay** still has its warehouses of 1907.

Custom Houses

The Custom House, by the riverside at **Greenock**, is one of the most prominent buildings in the town. The **Glasgow** Custom House is in Clyde Street, also by the riverside. The **Leith** Custom House is in Sandport.

Lighthouses

Arbroath Museum, situated in the signal tower of the **Bell Rock lighthouse**, has displays on its building. Most of the others are to be found at the extremities of the country. **Ardnamurchan**, on the most westerly point of the British mainland, has a visitor centre. **Kinnaird Head**, near **Fraserburgh**, is now Scotland's Lighthouse Museum. **Corsewall Point**, in the south-west, is a hotel. **Stromness Museum** in Orkney has displays on the many lighthouses in the area. At **Neist Point** in Skye, the keeper's cottages are available for holiday lets. **Bressay Lighthouse** in Shetland is being developed as a heritage centre. The **Gairloch Heritage Museum** in **Rosshire** has the lighthouse's lantern, reflectors and foghorn on display.

Offices

The **Clyde Navigation Trust** offices in Robertson Street, now the headquarters of Clyde Port Authority, were built from 1882 and have some of the grandest interiors in the city. The **Anchor Line Offices** in St Vincent Place, **Glasgow**, built in 1906-7, have many maritime motifs on the exterior.

Maritime Museums

The **Glasgow Museum of Transport** has a fine collection of models, many of ships that were used for transport in Scottish waters in the last century and a half. The **Scottish Fisheries Museum** at **Anstruther** is the main centre for fishing. **Aberdeen Maritime Museum** has outstanding displays on the North Sea oil industry and on local maritime history. The **Denny Test Tank, Dumbarton**, is part of the Scottish Maritime Museum. It is virtually the only part of the yard to survive, apart from the offices, and it is the oldest surviving tank in the world. The **Linthouse** building, part of the Scottish Maritime Museum at **Irvine**, was the engine shop of the Alexander Stephen shipyard. **Braehead**, on the Clyde near **Glasgow**, is a major new museum of Clyde shipbuilding. **The Scottish United Services Museum** in Edinburgh Castle has displays on Scottish naval history.

Monuments

The Napier engine from the steamer *Leven*, built in 1824, is situated just outside the **Denny Test Tank** in **Dumbarton**. The engine from the paddle tug *Clyde* is on the south bank of the Clyde near the **Renfrew Ferry**. Several cranes are preserved on the Clyde, at the **Fairfield yard, Finnieston, John Brown's** and **Scott Lithgow's**. All are of the hammerhead type, generally used in fitting out basins, or in the case of Finnieston, to put heavy items of cargo into ships.

Surviving shipyards

Little has been done to preserve old shipyard sites, compared with the efforts to save old docks, or naval dockyards. The former **John Browns** yard, now UIE, can best be seen from across the river at the mouth of the River Cart. Glimpses of **Fairfield**, now operated by GEC, can be had from across the river and the imposing entrance is in Govan Road. Building at **Yarrows** is largely done in sheds, and frigates fitting out can be seen from the river. **Ferguson** of **Port Glasgow** is next to Newark Castle.

Naval Bases

The **Martello Tower** in **Longhope Sound, Orkney**, was constructed in 1815 and modified in 1866. **Scapa Flow** still contains many relics of naval occupation, mostly defences from the Second World War; the wrecks of the *Vanguard* and *Royal Oak* are marked with buoys. **Stromness Museum** contains many salvaged relics of the High Seas Fleet. The **Churchill Barriers** form part of the road system of the islands; the wrecks that blocked the Sounds before the Barriers are mostly visible. The **Italian Chapel** is on the island of **Lamb Holm**. There is a naval museum in the former base at **Lyness**. **Rosyth Dockyard** is best seen from the Forth Road Bridge. The harbours at **Port Edgar** and **Granton** show a few traces of their former naval use. One of the best viewpoints of the Clyde is from **Lyle Hill, Greenock**, where there is a memorial to the Free French Navy. The **Clyde Submarine Base** at **Faslane** is definitely not open to the public. However, there are good views from across the Gareloch. In the **Holy Loch**, the war memorial at **Ardnadam** commemorates the submarines lost during voyages from the base.

Preserved ships

Mobile: *Carola*, steam yacht, built in 1898 by Scott of Bowling is based at **Irvine**. *Reaper*, a sailing Fifie fishing boat built in Sandhaven around 1900 is usually moored in **Anstruther Harbour**. *Sir Walter Scott*, built by Denny in 1899, operates in **Loch Katrine**. *Waverley*, built by A. and J. Inglis in 1946, the last of the Clyde paddle steamers, makes regular summer trips on the **Firth of Clyde**.

Puffers: Several puffers are in existence, all of the VIC type, built for the Navy during the Second World War to traditional puffer design. Many were built in England and *VIC 56* and *VIC 96* are based in **London** and **Maryport, Cumbria** respectively. *Spartan*, now in the **Scottish Maritime Museum, Irvine** featured in the most recent *Para Handy* series on television. *Auld Reekie* and *Vic 32* were built in England but operate in the **West of Scotland**.

Static Ships: *Antares*, a Carradale fishing boat dragged down by a Royal Navy submarine in 1990 with the loss of all hands, and later recovered, is now at **Irvine**. *Britannia*, former Royal Yacht was built by John Brown's in 1953 and is preserved in **Leith Harbour**. *Carrick*, ex *City of Adelaide* was built in 1864 in Sunderland, England as a full-rigged sailing ship; at present at **Irvine**, its future is in serious doubt. *Discovery*, Captain Scott's famous Polar exploration ship was built at Stephen's Yard in **Dundee** in 1901 and is now preserved in the city. *Explorer*, a trawler and fishery research vessel built in **Aberdeen** in 1955 is now a museum ship in the harbour. *Glenlee*, built in 1896 by A. Rodger of Port Glasgow as a barque rigged cargo ship is being preserved at **Yorklands Quay, Glasgow**, by the Clyde Maritime Trust. *Garnock*, a tugboat built in 1956 for the River Garnock by George Brown of Greenock and *Kyles*, a small coaster built in 1872 by Fullerton of Paisley are both now in the **Scottish Maritime Museum**. *North Carr* Lightship, built in 1933 by Inglis of Glasgow is now at **Anstruther**. *Renfrew Ferry*, the old chain ferry built in 1935 in Paisley, is preserved on the **south bank of the Clyde** next to its old station. *Unicorn*, a Royal Navy frigate built in 1824 in Chatham Dockyard, never put to sea except to be towed to **Dundee** in 1873. It is the oldest British-built warship afloat.

Bibliography

Adamnan, *Life of St Columba*, reprinted Lampeter, 1988.

Anon, *Orkneyinga Saga: the history of the Earls of Orkney*, Harmondsworth, 1981.

Baker, Richard, *The Terror of Tobermory*, London, 1972.

Butt, John, *The Industrial Archaeology of Scotland*, Newton Abbot, 1967.

Cavers, Keith, *A Vision of Scotland*, Edinburgh, 1993.

Coull, James R., *The Sea Fisheries of Scotland*, Edinburgh, 1996.

Davidson, J. and Gray, A. *The Scottish Staple at Veere*, London, 1909.

Defoe, Daniel, *A Tour Through the Whole Island of Great Britain*, reprinted Yale and London, 1991.

Devine, T. M., *The Tobacco Lords*, Edinburgh, 1975.

Devine, T. M. (ed.), *A Scottish Firm in Virginia*, Scottish History Society, Edinburgh, 1984.

Duckworth, C. L. D. and Langmuir, G. E., *Clyde River and other Steamers*, Glasgow, 1937.

Ereira, Alan, *The Invergordon Mutiny*, London, 1981.

Fairfield Shipbuilding and Engineering Company, *History of the Company, Review of its Productions and Description of the Works*, London, 1909.

Gibson, John S., *Ships of the '45*, London, 1967.

Hackmann, Willem, *Seek and Strike – Sonar, Anti-Submarine Warfare and the Royal Navy, 1914-54*, London, 1984.

Hay, Geoffrey D. and Stell, Geoffrey P., *Monuments of Industry*, Edinburgh, 1986.

Hewison, W. S., *This Great Harbour, Scapa Flow*, Kirkwall, 1985.

Hill, D. O. and Adamson, R. (Sara Stevenson (ed.)) *The Fishermen and Women of the Firth of Forth*, Edinburgh, 1991.

Hume, John R., *The Industrial Archaeology of Scotland*, 2 vols, Newton Abbot, 1976-7.

Hume Brown, P., *Early Travellers in Scotland*, Edinburgh, 1891.

Insh, George Pratt, *Darien Shipping Papers*, Scottish History Society, Edinburgh, 1924.

Jackson, Gordon, *The History and Archaeology of Ports*, Tadworth, 1983.

Johnson, Samuel and Boswell, James, *Journey to the Hebrides*, Edinburgh, 1996.

Kennedy, Ludovic, *On My Way to the Club*, London, 1989.

Lindsay, Alexander, *A Rutter of the Scottish Seas, circa 1540*, Greenwich, 1980.

Lyon, D. J., *The Denny List*, 4 vols, Greenwich, 1975.

McDonald, R. Andrew, *The Kingdom of the Isles*, East Linton, 1997.

McDonald, Dan, *The Clyde Puffer*, Newton Abbot, 1977.

Macdougall, Norman, *James IV*, Edinburgh, 1989.

McLellan, R. S., *Anchor Line 1856-1956*, Glasgow, 1956.

McCrorie, Ian, *Clyde Piers, a Pictorial History*, Greenock, 1982.

McCrorie, Ian, *Clyde Pleasure Steamers*, Greenock, 1986.

McCrorie, Ian, *Steamers of the Highlands and Islands*, Greenock, 1987.

Mannering, Julian (ed.), *The Chatham Directory of Inshore Craft*, London, 1997.

Martin, Colin, *Water Transport and the Roman Occupation of North Britain* in *Scotland and the Sea*, Smout (ed.), Edinburgh, 1992.

Marwick, Sir James D., *The River Clyde and the Clyde Burghs*, Glasgow, 1909.

Mowat, Robert C., *The Logboats of Scotland*, Oxford, 1996.

Munro, J. and R. W., *Acts of the Lords of the Isles, 1336-1493*, Scottish History Society, 1986.

Munro, R. W., *Scottish Lighthouses*, Stornaway, 1979.

Napier, David, *David Napier, Engineer, 1790-1869*, Glasgow, 1912.

Napier, James, *Life of Robert Napier of West Shandon*, Edinburgh, 1904.

Noble, Alexander, *The Scottish Inshore Fishing Boat*, Greenwich, 1978.

Paterson, J. S., *The Golden Years of the Clyde Steamers (1889-1914)*, Newton Abbot, 1969.

Paterson, Len, *The Light in the Glens*, Colonsay, 1996.

Peebles, Hugh B., *Warshipbuilding on the Clyde*, Edinburgh, 1987.

Pollard, Sidney and Robertson, Paul, *The British Shipbuilding Industry, 1870-1914*, Cambridge, Mass., 1979.

Prebble, John, *The Darien Disaster*, reprinted Edinburgh, 1978.

Reid, W. Stanford, *Sea-Power in the Anglo-Scottish War, 1296-1318* in *Mariners' Mirror*, vol. XLVI, 1960.

Ridell, John F, *Clyde Navigation*, Edinburgh, 1979.

Ritchie, Anna, *Viking Scotland*, London, 1993.

Rixson, Denis, *The West Highland Galley*, Edinburgh, 1998.

Roosenboom, M. O., *The Scottish Staple in the Netherlands*, The Hague, 1910.

Slaven, Anthony and Checkland, Sydney, *Dictionary of Scottish Business Biography, 1860-1960*, 2 vols, Aberdeen, 1986-90.

Smout, T. C., *Scottish Trade on the Eve of Union, 1660-1707*, Edinburgh, 1963.

Steer, K. A. and Bannerman, J. W. M., *Late Medieval Monumental Sculpture in the West Highlands*, Edinburgh, 1977.

Stephens, Alexander and Sons Ltd, *A Shipbuilding History 1750-1932*, London and Cheltenham, *c.* 1932.

Stevenson, Robert Louis, *The Amateur Emigrant, from the Clyde to Sandy Hook*, Chicago, 1895.

Stevenson, Thomas, *The Design and Construction of Harbours*, Edinburgh, 1864.

Thomas, John, *A Regional History of the Railways of Great Britain, Vol. IV, Scotland: The Lowlands and the Borders*, Newton Abbot, 1971.

Thomas, P. N., *British Steam Tugs*, Wolverhampton, 1983.

Turner, John R., *Scotland's North Sea Gateway*, Aberdeen, 1986.

Van der Vat, Dan, *The Grand Scuttle*, London, 1982.

Walker, Frank Arneil and Sinclair, Fiona J., *The North Clyde Estuary, an Illustrated Architectural Guide*, Edinburgh, 1992.

Walker, Fred M., *Song of the Clyde, a History of Clyde Shipbuilding*, Cambridge, 1984.

Williamson, Elizabeth, Riches, Anna and Higgs, Malcolm, *The Buildings of Scotland*, Glasgow, London, 1990.

Wilson, Gloria, *Scottish Fishing Boats*, Beverley, 1995.

Wickham-Jones, C. R., *Scotland's First Settlers*, London, 1994.

Index